CHINA
A General Survey

QI WEN

FOREIGN LANGUAGES PRESS   BEIJING

First Edition   1979
Second Edition   1981
Third (Revised) Edition   1984

ISBN   0-8351-1353-1

Published by the Foreign Languages Press
24 Baiwanzhuang Road, Beijing, China

Printed by the Foreign Languages Printing House
19 West Chegongzhuang Road, Beijing, China

Distributed by China International Book Trading Corporation
(Guoji Shudian), P.O. Box 399, Beijing, China

Printed in the People's Republic of China

The national flag of the People's Republic of China

The national emblem of the People's Republic of China

EDITOR'S NOTE

It has been 35 years since the founding of the People's Republic of China in 1949. The Chinese people, led by the Chinese Communist Party, have made remarkable progress in turning the old, backward and poverty-stricken China into a new socialist state, a state that has achieved initial prosperity, despite the many difficulties to overcome. However, for various reasons, the course of the Chinese people has been tortuous and the country has suffered many setbacks and even failures. China is now entering a new historical era which involves summing up the experiences and lessons of its socialist construction, and taking economic development as the main direction for future work. Confident of their success, people all over the country are striving to build the country into a modern socialist nation.

This book is not to give a comprehensive and detailed account of New China, but to provide the reader who is interested in China with the basic facts of China's current political, economic and cultural life and its brief history and geography. We hope it can serve as an introductory book for those who are interested in China.

CONTENTS

Chapter I GEOGRAPHY 1
1. Territory and Administrative Divisions 1
2. Topography 3
3. Mountains 3
4. Rivers and Lakes 7
5. Climate 8
6. Natural Resources 12
7. Population and Nationalities 13

Chapter II HISTORY 17
1. Antiquity to A.D. 1840 17
2. Modern History (1840-1919) 26
3. Contemporary History (1919-49) 31

Chapter III POLITICS 37
1. The Constitution of the People's Republic of China 37
2. The National People's Congress 40
3. The President of the State 45
4. The State Council 46
5. The Central Military Commission 51
6. The Local People's Congresses and the Local People's
   Governments at Different Levels 52
7. The People's Courts and the People's Procuratorates 56
8. Political Parties and People's Organizations 60
9. The Chinese People's Political Consultative Conference 69

Chapter IV ECONOMY 72
1. Agriculture 72
2. Industry 86
3. Communications and Transport 102
4. Money, Banking and Public Finance 115
5. Commerce and Tourist Industry 125
6. Foreign Trade 132

Chapter V CULTURE 146
1. Education 146
2. Science and Technology 153
3. Medical and Public Health Work 158
4. Sports 165
5. Literature and the Arts 172
6. The Press and Publications 189
7. Languages and Religion 196

Appendices 204
1. Countries Having Diplomatic Relations with China 204
2. Conversion Table 211
3. Distances by Rail Between China's Main Cities 212
4. A Brief Chinese Chronology 213
5. Time Difference Between Major Cities in the World 215

Chapter I

GEOGRAPHY

1. TERRITORY AND ADMINISTRATIVE DIVISIONS

China is situated in the eastern part of Asia, on the west coast of the Pacific Ocean.

Territory Third largest country in the world next to the Soviet Union and Canada, China has a total land area of 9.6 million square kilometres. It stretches from the central line of the main navigation channel of the Heilongjiang River near Mohe in the north (latitude 53° N.) to the Zengmu Reef of the Nansha Islands in the south (latitude 4° N.), and from the Pamirs to the west of Wuqia County in the Xinjiang Uygur Autonomous Region in the west (longitude 73° E.) to the confluence of the Heilongjiang and Wusuli rivers in the east (longitude 135° E.). China has a land boundary more than 20,000 kilometres long and is bordered by the Democratic People's Republic of Korea to the east; the People's Republic of Mongolia to the north; the Soviet Union to the northeast and northwest; Afghanistan, Pakistan, India, Nepal, Sikkim and Bhutan to the west and southwest; and Burma, Laos and Viet Nam to the south.

The Chinese mainland is flanked by the Bohai Sea, the Yellow Sea, the East China Sea and the South China Sea in the east and south. The Bohai Sea is an inland sea. The coastline of the mainland measures more than 18,000 kilometres. Across the East China Sea to the east and the South China Sea to the southeast, are Japan, the Philippines, Malaysia, Indonesia and Brunei. More than 5,000 islands are scattered over China's vast territorial seas, the largest being Taiwan and the next largest, Hainan. The numerous islands, islets, reefs and shoals dotting the South China Sea are collectively referred to as the South China Sea islands but individually known as the Dongsha, the Xisha, the Zhongsha and the Nansha islands.

Administrative Divisions For administrative purposes, China is divided into 22 provinces, 5 autonomous regions* and 3 municipalities directly under the Central Government.

The administrative units under a province or an autonomous region include cities, autonomous prefectures, counties, and autonomous counties. Under a county or an autonomous county are townships, nationality townships and towns.

The 22 provinces are: Hebei, Shanxi, Liaoning, Jilin, Heilongjiang, Shaanxi, Gansu, Qinghai, Shandong, Jiangsu, Zhejiang, Anhui, Jiangxi, Fujian, Taiwan, Henan, Hubei, Hunan, Guangdong, Sichuan, Guizhou and Yunnan.

The 5 autonomous regions are: the Inner Mongolia Autonomous Region, the Ningxia Hui Autonomous Region, the Xinjiang Uygur Autonomous Region, the Guangxi Zhuang Autonomous Region, and the Tibet Autonomous Region.

The 3 municipalities directly under the Central Government are Beijing, Shanghai and Tianjin.

Beijing, the capital of China, is situated to the west of the Bohai Sea and on the northwest fringe of the North China Plain. Covering an area of 16,800 square kilometres with a population of 9.23 million (in 1982), it is the country's political, economic, scientific and cultural centre, as well as the hub of its communications network. An ancient capital with a history of 800 years, it contains many scenic spots and places of historical interest.

*See pp. 16, 38 and 52.

2. TOPOGRAPHY

China's topography is varied and slopes from west to east. From the air, China's topographical outline looks like a staircase moving from west to east, descending step by step from the Qinghai-Tibet Plateau to the coastal area in the east.

The Qinghai-Tibet Plateau, the top of the staircase, covers 2.2 million square kilometres and averages 4,000 metres above sea level. It is the highest and largest plateau on earth and is popularly called "Roof of the World".

From the eastern and northern rims of the Qinghai-Tibet Plateau, the terrain drops abruptly to between 2,000 and 1,000 metres above sea level, forming the second step down the staircase with the Junggar, the Tarim and the Sichuan basins, and the Inner Mongolia, the Loess and the Yunnan-Guizhou plateaus.

Crossing the stretch of mountain area on the eastern margin of the second step of the staircase, namely, the Greater Hinggan, the Taihang, the Wushan, the Wuling and the Xuefeng mountains, to the sea coast, the land drops to less than 500 metres above sea level to form the third step down the staircase. Here, lying from north to south, are the Northeast China Plain, the North China Plain, the Middle-Lower Yangtze River Plain and the Pearl River Delta. Foothills and hilly country border these plains.

To the east of the third step are the shallows, which are an extension of the land into the sea. The depth of this water is, as a rule, less than 200 metres.

3. MOUNTAINS

China is famous for its many mountains which comprise more than two-thirds of its total land area. They fall into three groups according to the direction in which they run, namely, the east-west, the northeast-southwest, and the north-south ranges.

CHINA'S MOUNTAINS

Lesser Hinggan Mts.

Greater Hinggan Mts.

Changbai Mts.

Tianshan Mts.

Yanshan Mts.

Taihang Mts.

Dabie Mts.

Taiwan Mts.

Wuyi Mts.

Yanshan Mts.

Liupan Mts.

Daba Mts.

Xuefeng Mts.

Nanling Mts.

Helan Mts.

Qinling Mts.

Dalou Mts.

Qilian Mts.

Hengduan Mts.

Altay Mts.

Altun Mts.

Bayan 'Har Mts.

Tanggula Mts.

Tianshan Mts.

Kunlun Mts.

Hoh xil Mts.

Gangdise Mts.

Karakorum Mts.

Himalayas

South China Sea Is.

0   250   500   750 km.

The east-west ranges, mainly in the western part of China, include the Altay, the Tianshan, the Kunlun, the Karakorum, the Gangdise, the Himalayas, the Qinling, and the Nanling.

The Altay, meaning "the Golden Mountains" in Mongolian, are in the northern part of the Xinjiang Uygur Autonomous Region and have an average height of 3,000 metres above sea level. This range runs southeastwards to the People's Republic of Mongolia.

The Tianshan Mountains running across the middle of Xinjiang are 3,000 to 5,000 metres above sea level, the highest peaks in the west of the Tianshan chain reaching 7,000 metres. The mountain massif is made up of several parallel ranges with depressed basins in between. The water level of the Aydingkol Lake in the centre of the Turpan Depression is 154 metres below sea level and is the lowest-lying area in China.

The Kunlun Mountains, starting from the Pamirs in the west, extend eastwards 2,500 kilometres to the northwestern part of the Sichuan Basin. On the whole, they are over 5,000 metres above sea level, and a number of peaks reach 7,000 metres in height. Melting ice from the stupendous peaks of the Kunlun chain feeds the Yellow River and the Yangtze River. The Bayan Har Mountains which are the east section of the Kunlun form the watershed for these two rivers.

The Qinling extends about 1,500 kilometres across central China from southern Gansu in the west to the area between the lower reaches of the Huaihe River and the Yangtze River in the east. Rising 2,000-3,000 metres above sea level, this massif forms the watershed between the catchment areas of the two rivers.

The Karakorum, meaning "the Purplish Black Kunlun" in Uygur, starts from the Xinjiang-Kashmir border in the northwest and stretches southeastwards into the northern part of Tibet. The average height of the range is 6,000 metres above sea level, while the Qogir, its main peak, reaches 8,611 metres in elevation, making it the second highest summit in the world.

The Nanling Range includes all the mountains between Guangxi-Guangdong and Hunan-Jiangxi provinces. It consists of the Yuecheng, the Dupang, the Mengzhu, the Qitian, and the Dayu mountains. This group is also known as the Five Mountains.

The Gangdise, meaning "Master of All Mountains" in Tibetan, towers 6,000 metres above sea level over southern Tibet to form the watershed between rivers of the continental plateau drainage system and those of the Indian Ocean drainage system. Its main peak, the Kangrinboqe, meaning "Treasure of the Snow", is a sacred mountain visited by Buddhist pilgrims.

The Himalayas rise above the southern rim of the Qinghai-Tibet Plateau, the main part of the range lying on the Sino-Indian and Sino-Nepalese borders. The 2,500-kilometre mountain chain averages 6,000 metres above sea level, although more than 40 precipitous, snow-capped peaks are upwards of 7,000 metres in elevation. The main peak, Mount Qomolangma (or "Goddess Peak" in Tibetan) of the Himalayas — which itself means "Abode of Snow" in Sanskrit — soars 8,848.13 metres above sea level of the Sino-Nepalese border. It is the highest mountain in the world. Chinese mountaineers twice, in 1960 and 1975, climbed to the summit of Qomolangma from the north face and conducted multi-disciplinary research work in the region.

The northeast-southwest ranges, composed of an eastern and a western chain, are located mainly in the eastern part of China. The former includes the Changbai Mountains in northeast China, averaging 2,700 metres in elevation, and ranges of mountains of some 1,000 metres above sea level stretching across the Liaodong and the Shandong peninsulas down south to Zhejiang and Fujian provinces. The western chain is composed of the Greater Hinggan Range in northeast China, the Taihang Mountains in north China, the heights along the Yangtze River Gorges and the Xuefeng Mountains in Hunan.

The north-south ranges include the Hengduan Mountains in

western Sichuan and Yunnan provinces and the mountains in eastern Taiwan Province. The former includes the Daxue, the Nushan and the Gaoligong mountains, averaging 4,500 to 5,000 metres above sea level, and its highest peak, the Gongga, soaring 7,590 metres above sea level. This range blocks communication between east and west — hence its name Hengduan, meaning "Barrier Mountains" in Chinese. The 3,950-metre Mount Yushan in eastern Taiwan Province is the highest peak in southeast China.

4. RIVERS AND LAKES

Rivers China has a great number of rivers, more than 1,500 of which have a catchment area exceeding 1,000 square kilometres. Among these, the Yangtze River, Yellow River, Heilongjiang River, Pearl River, Haihe River, and Huaihe River are the major ones.

The Yangtze River, the longest river in China and the third longest in the world, originates as the Tuotuo River on the southwestern side of the snow-draped Geladandong, the main peak of the Tanggula Mountains. It flows through Qinghai, Tibet, Sichuan, Yunnan, Hubei, Hunan, Jiangxi, Anhui and Jiangsu and empties into the East China Sea at Shanghai. It has a total length of 6,300 kilometres and a catchment area of 1,807,199 square kilometres, and is an arterial waterway connecting such important cities as Shanghai, Nanjing, Wuhan and Chongqing. During the high-water season, 10,000-ton ships can sail as far inland as Wuhan.

The Yellow River is the second longest river in China. Originating from the north face of the Bayan Har Mountains of Qinghai, it flows through Qinghai, Sichuan, Gansu, Ningxia, Inner Mongolia, Shaanxi, Shanxi, Henan and Shandong and empties into the Bohai Sea at Kenli County in Shandong. It has a total length of 5,464 kilometres and a catchment area of more than 752,443 square kilometres. On its banks lie Lanzhou, Baotou, Zhengzhou, Jinan and other impor-

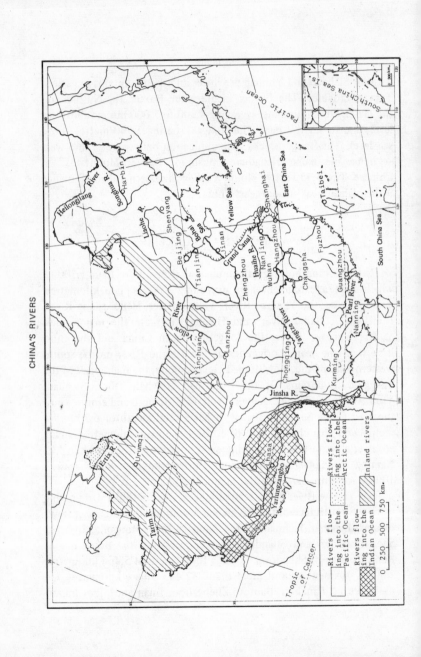

CHINA'S RIVERS

Pacific Ocean

Heilongjiang
Songhua R.
River R.
Harbin

Liaohe R.
Shenyang

Bohai Sea
Beijing
Tianjin
Grand Canal
Jinan
Yellow Sea
Qingdao
Shanghai
East China Sea
Taibei

Zhengzhou
Huaihe R.
Nanjing
Wuhan
Hangzhou
Fuzhou

Yellow
River
Lanzhou
Changsha
Guangzhou
Pearl River
Nanning

Yinchuan

Chongqing
Yangze River

Kunming

South China Sea

Jinsha R.

Ertix R.
Urumqi

Lhasa
Yarlungzangbo R.

Tarim R.

Tropic of Cancer

Rivers flow-
ing into the
Pacific Ocean

Rivers flow-
ing into the
Indian Ocean

Rivers flow-
ing into the
Arctic Ocean

Inland rivers

0   250   500   750 km.

South China Sea IS.
300 km.

tant cities. The Yellow River valley is considered the cradle of Chinese civilization.

The Pearl River is the largest river in southern China. Of its three main tributaries — the Xijiang, Beijiang and Dongjiang — the Xijiang is the longest, rising in the Wumeng mountain area of Yunnan to flow through Guizhou and Guangxi and empty into the South China Sea in Guangdong Province. It is 2,197 kilometres long and its large flow makes it a fine navigable river.

Most of the rivers in China's northwest basins and plateau areas are inland rivers, supplied by alpine melt water. Because of excessive evaporation and percolation, they are small, seasonal and intermittent streams. The Tarim River of Xinjiang, however, fed incessantly by the abundant melt water of the Tianshan, the Kunlun and the Pamirs, is a well-known inland river of more than 2,000 kilometres in length.

China also has many large canals, such as the Beijing-Hangzhou Grand Canal that links north to south, and the Hunan-Guangxi Canal connecting the Yangtze River water system with that of the Pearl River.

Lakes There are 370 sizable lakes, 130 of which exceed 100 square kilometres in area, in addition to many man-made lakes and reservoirs.

Most of the lakes are found on the Middle-Lower Yangtze River Plain and the Yunnan-Guizhou Plateau. There are also a large number on the Qinghai-Tibet Plateau, in the Inner Mongolia-Xinjiang region and northeast China. China's big size, complex land forms and diverse climate give each lake special characteristics.

If, according to the characteristics of the lakes, a diagonal line were drawn across China from the southern section of the Greater Hinggan Range through the Yinshan and the eastern section of the Qilian mountain chain to the Gangdise massif, most of the salt lakes would fall northwest of this line. These lakes in the interior drainage basins have little water and no outlets, but they are rich in raw chemical materials, such as salt and alkali. Best known among them are the Qinghai Lake, the Nam Co and the Siling Co on the Qinghai-Tibet Plateau and the Lop Nur of Xinjiang. The lakes southeast of the diagonal line would be mostly fresh-water ones. As they are situated in the exterior drainage basins, they have outlets through rivers. These lakes provide inland water transport and irrigation, are a source of fertilizer and support fresh-water fish farming. Some of them are also famous as health resorts and tourist sites. Best known among the fresh-water lakes are the Dongting, Honghu, Poyang, Chaohu, Taihu and Yangcheng on the Middle-Lower Yangtze River Plain; the Baiyang, Weishan and Hongze on the Yellow-Huaihe-Haihe River Plain; and the Dianchi and Erhai on the Yunnan-Guizhou Plateau. The better known lakes in northeast China are the Jingbo and Hulun, and Lake Xingkai, which straddles the Sino-Soviet border.

5. CLIMATE

China is situated in the southeastern part of the Eurasian continent, on the west coast of the Pacific. The country's location puts its climate under the influence of the monsoonal winds. Great differences in climate are found from region to region owing to its extensive territory and complex topography.

Leizhou Peninsula, Hainan Island and the South China Sea islands of Guangdong Province, Taiwan Province and the southern part of Yunnan Province have a tropical climate, where summer reigns all the year round, giving rise to verdant and luxuriant vegetation. Heilongjiang Province in the northeast has a short and cool summer and a severe winter. The area around the Yangtze River and Huaihe River valleys in the east is warm and humid with four distinct seasons. The Inner Mongolia-Xinjiang area in the northwest experiences extremities of weather in a single day. The saying, "Fur coats

Hainan Island.

The 8,848.13-metre-high Mount Qomolangma, the world's highest peak, on the Sino-Nepalese border.

The Sisters' Pool (*above*), and the Lake of Sun and Moon (*below*) in the Ali Mountains, Taiwan Province.

Rippling sea of sand, Taklimakan Desert, northwest China.

Lumbering in the Greater Hinggan Mountains, northeast China.

Mount Huangshan.

Lijiang River, Guangxi Zhuang Autonomous Region.

One of the three picturesque Yangtze River gorges.

The Huangguoshu Waterfall, Guizhou Province.

in the morning and gossamer at noon," gives a true picture of this parched area. Some areas of the Yunnan-Guizhou Plateau in China's southwest have a mild winter and cool summer, as does Kunming, which is justly named "the City of Spring" as its weather is like spring the whole year through. The Tibet Plateau has a cold, dry climate and a strong sun. In some mountain areas with deep narrow gorges, pronounced differences in climate are found between high and low altitudes. In general, however, China lies mainly in the northern temperate zone and has four recognizable seasons with high temperatures and heavy rainfall alternating with low temperatures and scanty rainfall.

Annual Temperature Difference of China's Major Cities

City	Average January temperature	Average July temperature	Annual difference
Beijing	-4.8°C	25.8°C	30.6°C
Shanghai	3.5°C	28°C	24.5°C
Qingdao	-1.1°C	23.7°C	24.8°C
Guangzhou	13.7°C	28.3°C	14.6°C
Wuhan	2.7°C	29.1°C	26.4°C
Urumqi	-15.8°C	23.9°C	39.7°C
Shenyang	-13°C	24.9°C	37.9°C

As shown in the chart, the temperature difference between north and south is vast in winter, but slight in summer. The January

temperature difference between Harbin in the northeast and Guangzhou in the south is 35°C. When the area around the Songhua River
is still covered in snow, spring has already entered the Pearl River
valley. July, however, is the swimming season in both regions as the
temperature difference during this month is only 5°C. Waterproof
garments are indispensable in southeast China, whereas in many
parts of the northwest they are unnecessary. This shows the gradual
decrease in precipitation from the southeast to the northwest.

6. NATURAL RESOURCES

China's territory covers the frigid, temperate and tropical zones
and encompasses a wide variety of ecospheres, giving it with rich
natural resources.

The diversity of China's natural flora and fauna is tremendous.

Fauna   According to the statistics of 1976, China has 1,166
species of birds, comprising 13.5 per cent of the world's total; 421
species of mammals, amounting to 11.3 per cent of the known
species of the world; and 299 species of reptiles and 184 species of
amphibians. Wildlife particular to China include such well-known
animals as the giant panda, snub-nosed monkey, takin, white-lipped
deer, eared pheasant, Chinese river dolphin, Chinese alligator and
Chinese crocodile.

Flora   China has more than 32,000 species of higher plants,
among which over 2,000 species are food plants, and more than
2,800 species of trees, in addition to numerous species of herbal
plants used in preparing Chinese medicines. Apart from such traditional economic plants as cotton, soya bean, rapeseed, sugar-beet,
sugar-cane, tung oil and tea, tropical crops such as rubber, coffee, oil
palm, sisal hemp, cacao and pepper are also grown.

Minerals   China possesses great mineral wealth. It has coal deposits of various types, petroleum resources with low sulphur

content, widely distributed iron-ore deposits, and many non-ferrous metals including copper, aluminium, tungsten, antimony, molybdenum, tin, manganese, lead, zinc and mercury, whose reserves rank high in the world, as well as large quantities of oil shale, phosphorus, sulphur, magnesite, salt and gypsum reserves. Initial surveys put the country's coal reserves at 640,000 million tons. Iron-ore resources in the country are put at 44,000 million tons. Petroleum resources are fairly widely distributed over the land of China, and the country's continental shelves are also rich in oil.

Almost all the major minerals in the world have been found in China. In recent years, new deposits have been discovered.

The total outflow of all the rivers in China is more than 2,700 billion cubic metres, and the total water power reserves reach 680 million kw., ranking first in the world.

7. POPULATION AND NATIONALITIES

Population According to the Third Population Census of 1982, the total population of China is 1,031,882,511 on July 1, 1982, 22.6 per cent of the world's total population, making China the world's most populous country. The population of the 29 mainland provinces, municipalities directly under the Central Government and autonomous regions (excluding Jinmen and Mazu islands of Fujian Province) is 1,018,175,288, with women making up 48.5 per cent and men, 51.5 per cent. The urban population is 206,588,582, 20.6 per cent of the total population, a 2.2 per cent increase over the Second Population Census of 1964.

China's population is unevenly distributed, the inland areas more sparsely populated and coastal provinces densely populated. According to the statistics of this population census, the population density per square kilometre is 107 people, 33 more than in the Second Population Census of 1964. The population density of the

7 coastal provinces, 3 municipalities and an autonomous region has risen from 232.7 people per square kilometre in 1964 to 320.6 people in 1982. For the 14 inland provinces and 4 autonomous regions, the population density has increased from 47.3 people per square kilometre in 1964 to 71.4 people in 1982. Of these inland provinces and autonomous regions, the population density of sparsely populated Tibet, Qinghai, Xinjiang, Gansu, Ningxia and Inner Mongolia has risen from 7.2 people per square kilometre to 11.8 people.

In the first 20 years after the founding of New China, the population increased rapidly. At the beginning of the 1970s, China began to implement the policy of planned population control and the national growth rate dropped noticeably from 26 per thousand in 1970 to 14.4 per thousand in 1982. The Chinese Government requires that the population of China be kept below 1.2 billion by the end of this century.

Population Growth from 1949 to 1983
(in millions)

Year	1949	1952	1957	1970	1979	1983
Population	541.67	574.82	646.53	825.42	970.92	1,024.95

Nationalities China is a unified, multi-national country with 56 enthnic groups. The Han nationality have the largest number of people – 936 million, or 93.3 per cent of China's total population. The population of the other 55 ethnic minority groups adds up to 67.23 million, or 6.7 per cent of China's population. The ethnic minority groups with people exceeding one million include: Mongolian, Hui, Tibetan, Uygur, Miao, Yi, Zhuang, Bouyei, Korean, Manchu, Tujia, Dong, Yao, Bai and Hani, 15 ethnic groups in all. Those with a population exceeding 100,000 are the Dai, Kazak, Li,

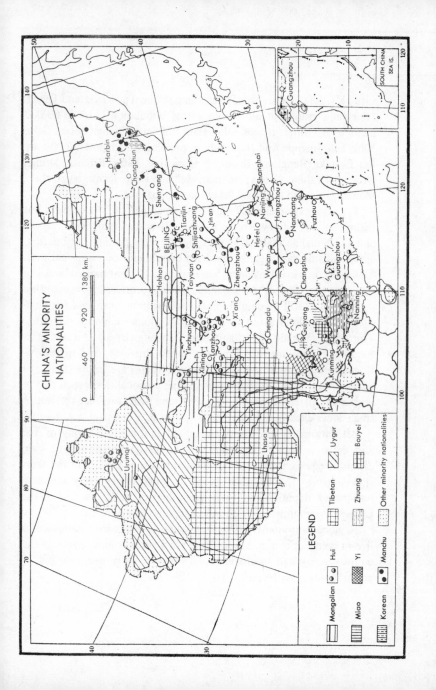

CHINA'S MINORITY NATIONALITIES

LEGEND

Mongolian
Hui
Miao
Korean
Manchu

Tibetan
Yi
Uygur
Zhuang
Bouyei
Other minority nationalities

0   460   920   1380 km.

Lisu, Va, She, Lahu, Shui, Dongxiang, Naxi, Tu, Kirgiz and Qiang, 13 ethnic groups in all. Those whose population exceeds 50,000 include 7 ethnic groups: the Daur, Mulam, Blang, Salar, Gelo, Xibe and Jingpo. And those whose population is below 50,000 are the Ewenki, Benglong, Bonan, Yugur, Jing, Tatar, Russian, Drung, Oroqen, Hezhen, Lhoba, Maonan, Achang, Pumi, Tajik, Nu, Ozbek, Moinba, Jino and Gaoshan, 20 ethnic groups in all.

The Han nationality is found living in all parts of the country but mainly in the Yellow River, Yangtze River and Pearl River valleys and the Songliao Plain of the northeast, while the minority nationalities inhabit vast regions that have been their home for centuries. There are, however, instances where many different nationalities live mingled together or as separate, widely scattered communities. According to still incomplete data, two or more than two nationalities commingle in about 70 per cent of China's counties and cities. Thirteen nationalities inhabit the Xinjiang Uygur Autonomous Region, 23 nationalities live in Yunnan Province, and in the Xishuangbanna Autonomous Prefecture there are more than 10 nationalities. The distribution of China's nationalities is such that in large areas different nationalities are found living together whereas in small areas each nationality tends to live in a compact community.

All nationalities in China are united in one great family of free and equal nations. They take part in the administration of state affairs as equals, irrespective of their numbers or the size of the areas they inhabit. The National People's Congress has many minority nationality deputies and there are minority leading cadres in the Chinese Communist Party and the People's Government.

Regional autonomy is practised where the minority nationalities live in compact communities. There are 5 autonomous regions in the country equivalent to provinces, 30 autonomous prefectures, and 75 autonomous counties (banners).

Chapter II

HISTORY

The Chinese civilization is one of the world's earliest. The country has found valuable remains of ancient cultures and has almost 4,000 years of written history.

1. ANTIQUITY TO A.D. 1840

Peking Man According to existing archaeological data, primitive men lived on the land about a million years ago. Fossils of the ape-man were discovered in Yuanmou, Yunnan Province (Yuanmou Man) and in Lantian, Shaanxi Province (Lantian Man). These were the earliest primitive men known in China. About 400,000 to 500,000 years ago, Peking Man, the ape-man who lived and worked around Zhoukoudian near Beijing, already possessed the basic characteristics of man: he could walk erect, make and use simple tools and knew how to use fire.

The Yangshao Culture and the Longshan Culture China went through the historical stages of the matriarchal clan commune and the patriarchal clan commune. The Yangshao Culture of 6,000-7,000 years ago was representative of the former while the Longshan Culture of 5,000 years ago was representative of the latter. During this period, people were already able to make stone tools for many purposes and had invented pottery. Apart from hunting and fishing, agriculture and animal husbandry had appeared. There is evidence of the phenomenon of class differences in the latter part of this period.

In the latter period of the primitive clan society, there were many tribes scattered in the Yellow River valley, among which the tribe headed by Huangdi was the most powerful with a fairly high culture. Huangdi was later regarded in Chinese mythology as the forefather of the Chinese nation.

Xia (c. 21st-16th centuries B.C.), Shang (c. 16th-11th century B.C.) and Western Zhou (c. 11th century-770 B.C.) According to tradition, Xia was the first dynasty in Chinese history.

The Xia gradually declined and was replaced by the Shang Dynasty which saw the development of a slave society. Agriculture and animal husbandry expanded to a certain extent. The techniques of sericulture, silk reeling and silk weaving were mastered. Bronze smelting and casting reached a fairly high level. A relatively fixed form of writing also came into existence. Oracle-bone inscriptions and inscriptions on bronzes told, among other things, of the activities of slaves. In Shang Dynasty tombs, immolated slaves were generally found buried beside their masters.

During the Western Zhou, after the Shang, slave society underwent further development. Agricultural production expanded and even breweries were set up.

Spring and Autumn Period (770-476 B.C.) and Warring States Period (475-221 B.C.) The Western Zhou ended in 770 B.C. and the Eastern Zhou began when the rulers moved their capital to Luoyi (present-day Luoyang, Henan Province). The reign of the Eastern Zhou is generally divided into two periods: the Spring and Autumn Period and the Warring States Period. These was a transitional phase from slave to feudal society. As iron smelting gradually developed, farm tools such as iron axes and hoes were made. Ploughing with oxen was introduced and the area of cultivatable land extended. With the development of the economy, relations of production under the slave system increasingly proved to be a restraint on new productive forces. The rule of the slave-owners was continuously challenged and the rising landlord class gradually replaced the slave-owning class. A new system of exploitation superseded the old one, but historically it had progressive significance.

There were radical social changes between the Spring and Autumn Period and the Warring States Period. Historical records show that there were over 140 princely states during the Spring and Autumn Period, but by the time of the Warring States only seven major states — Qi, Chu, Yan, Zhao, Han, Wei and Qin — survived, and among them there were intense struggles. Acute social changes were reflected in the ideological sphere in the conflicts between different schools of thought, with Confucius and Mencius representing the Confucian School, Mozi the Mohist School, Laozi and Zhuangzi the Taoist School, and Shang Yang and Han Fei the Legalist School. Literature and the arts also developed during the Warring States Period. A new style of poems and songs appeared in the south called the Chu Ci (Ballads of Chu), whose representative work was the famous *Li Sao* by the poet Qu Yuan.

China's feudal society lasted a long time and may be divided into various stages of development. Feudal separatism did exist at a certain time but the main trend was unity. With the passing of time, friendship and unity between China's various nationalities became ever closer.

The 700 years or so (475 B.C.-A.D. 220) from the Warring States to the end of the Eastern Han was a period when feudal society was established and consolidated. Remnants of the slave system were still found in different places and to differing degrees.

Qin Dynasty (221-207 B.C.) In 221 B.C., Qin Shi Huang (First Emperor of the Qin Dynasty) ended the separatism of the Warring States Period and established the first centralized, unified multi-national feudal state in Chinese history — the Qin Dynasty. He promoted feudal land-ownership, developed communications and unified the written language, currency, and weights and measures. All this helped the feudal system to develop. Qin Shi Huang, however, did not live to consolidate his empire.

Western Han (206 B.C.-A.D. 24) and Eastern Han (25-220) The
Western Han Dynasty was established by Liu Bang who, after a very
long period, consolidated the centralized landlord state. In the early
period of the Western Han Dynasty, agriculture and handicrafts
made good progress. The use of iron farm tools and ploughing with
oxen were widely adopted, farming techniques improved and many
irrigation projects built. Iron smelting and silk weaving were also
developed. Commerce flourished, foreign trade prospered and a
number of important cities sprang up. The latter period of the
Western Han was characterized by political decline and the sharpen-
ing of social contradictions. In A.D. 25 Liu Xiu, an educated landlord and a member of the Han royal house, established the Eastern
Han Dynasty, during which the feudal economy continued to
develop while various kinds of contradictions deepened.

The Qin, Western and Eastern Han dynasties, unable to resolve
growing social contradictions, were successively toppled by peasant
uprisings. The uprising led by Chen Sheng and Wu Guang in 209
B.C., the uprisings of the Lu Lin (Greenwood) Army and the Chi
Mei (Red Eye-Brows) Army in A.D. 17-18, and the uprising of the
Huang Jin (Yellow Turbans) in A.D. 184 were the largest peasant
revolts in a period of nearly 700 years. They overthrew the three
dynasties and dealt heavy blows to the landlord class.

Great achievements in science and culture were attained in the
Han Dynasty. The famous historian Sima Qian wrote the first
complete general history of China in his *Shi Ji* (*Records of the
Historian*). The distinguished thinker Wang Chong wrote *Lun Heng*
(*Discourses Weighed in the Balance*), in which he interpreted various
natural phenomena from a rudimentary materialist viewpoint. Zhang
Heng invented a seismograph and various astronomical instruments
moved by water power. The physician Zhang Zhongjing wrote *Shang
Han Lun* (*A Treatise on Fevers*), which has an important place in the
history of medicine. Silk fabrics were already well known to the

world during the Han Dynasty. The wife of Chen Baoguang of the Western Han invented a device to weave raised designs on fine silk, improving the techniques for manufacturing silk fabrics. The invention of paper was another major contribution of this period. Primitive paper had appeared as early as the Western Han, but Cai Lun of the Eastern Han, improving on the techniques of his forebears, used bark, bast fibre and pieces of cloth as material to make a better paper.

Three Kingdoms (220-80), Jin (265-420), Southern and Northern Dynasties (420-589), Sui (581-618) and Tang (618-907) After the Eastern Han, the 700 years from the Three Kingdoms of Wei, Shu and Wu, through unification under the Jin and the rival Southern and Northern Dynasties to unification under the Sui and Tang dynasties were an era of further development of feudal society. The characteristics of feudal relations in this period were the increasing acquisition of larger estates by landlords and monasteries with hereditary privileges and the increase of incidence of peasants bound to the land. During the Jin and the Southern and Northern Dynasties, relations among some nationalities in the north improved after a period of struggle, enabling economic development there to move ahead. Soon after, the economy of the south caught up. The rulers of the Sui had the Grand Canal dug from Luoyang to Hangzhou, which preceded the later north-south Grand Canal from Beijing to Hangzhou. It played an important role in the development of the economy. Farming techniques, production tools and water conservancy improved rapidly during the Tang Dynasty.

Zu Chongzhi, the outstanding scientist of the Southern and Northern Dynasties, in establishing the ratio between the circumference and diameter of a circle, worked out the precise figure of π to be between 3.1415926 and 3.1415927. Jia Sixie of the same period wrote *Qi Min Yao Shu* (*The Manual of Important Arts for the People*), which was a guide to agricultural and animal husbandry. Metallurgy made new advances as Qiwu Huaiwen introduced the

~~od~~ of pouring molten pig iron on wrought iron to smelt it into
~~-quality~~ steel. Buddhism was introduced into China during the
Eastern Han and flourished during the Southern and Northern
Dynasties, winning many followers among the ruling class. The great
thinker Fan Zhen wrote *Shen Mie Lun* (*Extinction of the Soul*),
sharply criticizing religious beliefs from an atheist viewpoint.

The Sui and Tang dynasties saw remarkable accomplishments in
science and culture. The architect Li Chun designed and built the
Zhaozhou Bridge (in present-day Zhaoxian County, Hebei Province),
the oldest stone-arch bridge in the world, over which traffic still
passes today. The monk Yi Xing was the first scientist in the world
to ascertain the length of the meridian line. Sun Simiao, versed in
medicine and pharmacology, wrote *Qian Jin Fang* (*Golden Prescriptions*), in which he recorded a great number of drugs and prescriptions. Gunpowder had been invented quite early; it began to be used
for warfare late in the Tang Dynasty. Wood-block printing, invented
by the Chinese, came into use in the Tang Dynasty, earlier than
anywhere else in the world.

Literature and art flourished with the famous poets Li Bai, Du
Fu, Li He, Li Shangyin, Bai Juyi, and the painter Wu Daozi.

Peasant uprisings in the last years of the Sui and the one led by
Huang Chao in the late Tang, the two largest in a period of 700
years, put an end to the rule of both dynasties. They shook the
foundations of the landlord class and paved the way for further
development of social productive forces.

**Five Dynasties (907-60), Song (960-1279) and Yuan (1271-
1368)** In the 460 years from the divided Five Dynasties, through
the co-existence of the Liao (916-1125), Song, Western Xia (1038-
1227) and Kin (1115-1234) to unification again under the Yuan,
feudal relations underwent marked changes. Hereditary land ownership was reduced and the bondage of peasants greatly decreas-
ed. The landlord class enlarged their land-holdings by purchases,
and exploited the peasants mainly by renting out land and collect-

ing rent in kind.

Agriculture, handicrafts, science and culture continued to develop. Cotton was planted for the first time in China and the textile industry grew. A woman labourer by the name of Huang Daopo improved the technique of cotton spinning and weaving. The agronomists Chen Fu and Wang Zhen wrote *Nong Shu* (*A Treatise on Agriculture*), which reflected the progress in farming. Printing improved with the introduction of movable type by Bi Sheng. The compass, an earlier invention, began to be used in navigation in the late 11th century. Summarizing the experiences accumulated by workers in building construction, Li Jie wrote *Ying Zao Fa Shi* (*Building Formulas*). Shen Kuo's *Meng Xi Bi Tan* (*Notes Written in Dream Brook Garden*) included researches into many aspects of physics, biology and geology. Guo Shoujing compiled a new calendar called *Shou Shi Li* (*Time-Telling Calendar*); he also invented many astronomical instruments and made contributions to the construction of irrigation works. New forms of literature appeared, such as the ballads of the Song and the plays of the Yuan. Well-known authors included Su Shi, Li Qingzhao, Xin Qiji, Lu You, Guan Hanqing and Wang Shifu.

Domestic and foreign trade flourished during the Song and Yuan; merchants and travellers came from abroad. The Venetian Marco Polo travelled widely in China, and in his *Travels* he described China's wealth and power and its thriving industry and trade. The Moroccan Ibn Batuta also visited and wrote about China's social conditions.

There were many peasant uprisings during this period. Peasant forces made political and economic demands for equality between the high and the low, the rich and the poor, marking a new stage of peasant revolts in the feudal age. The Yuan Dynasty collapsed under the impact of a peasant uprising, the largest of that period.

Ming (1368-1644) and Qing (1644-1911)   The period from the early Ming to the middle Qing, that is, from about 1368 to 1840,

saw the gradual decline of feudalism in China. Though the system
declined, the economy was still growing stronger. During the Ming,
agriculture and handicrafts made definite progress and rudiments of
capitalism appeared by the end of the Ming rule. In some textile and
iron-smelting works where the work was all manually done and
production was on a relatively large scale, job specialization appeared and workers were hired.

China during the Ming and Qing was already a united multi-
national country. The Qing territory extended to Lake Balkhash and
the Pamirs in the west and bordered Siberia in the north. In the
northeast, its frontier ran along the Outer Hinggan Range right up to
the sea (including the Island of Sakhalin). In the east was the Pacific
(including Taiwan and the nearby islands), and in the south the
frontier encompassed the Nansha Islands. The southwest embraced
Tibet and Yunnan. On this vast territory economic and cultural relations between the united nationalities were very close. From the
latter half of the 16th century, tsarist Russia did all it could to
expand its influence to Siberia. In the middle of the 17th century, it
invaded the Heilongjiang basin which had always been under the
administration of the Chinese government. The Qing Emperor
Kangxi (1662-1722) effectively blocked Russia's expansionist
movements. In 1689 China and Russia negotiated on the basis of
equality and concluded the Treaty of Nipchu which legally affirmed
that the extensive areas of the Heilongjiang and Wusuli basins were
China's territory.

There were great achievements in science and culture during the
Ming and Qing. Li Shizhen compiled *Ben Cao Gang Mu* (*Materia
Medica*), recording 1,800 kinds of medicine and some 10,000
prescriptions. His work was later translated into many foreign
languages. Summarizing his experience in agricultural and handicraft
production, Song Yingxing of the late Ming wrote *Tian Gong Kai Wu*
(*The Exploitation of the Works of Nature*), a work which reflects
the scientific and technical level of his time. Li Zhi, a 16th-century

progressive thinker, wrote treatises exposing and criticizing Confucian dogma which fettered people's thinking. Wang Fuzhi, who lived from the end of the Ming to the beginning of the Qing, was a proponent of historical evolution and opposed retrogression. During the two dynasties some long novels of a fairly high artistic standard appeared, the best known of which is *Hong Lou Meng* (*A Dream of Red Mansions*) by Cao Xueqin.

As feudal society approached its end, class contradictions grew increasingly acute. In scale and frequency and the extent to which they attracted other social strata, peasant uprisings in this period surpassed all previous ones. The best known was the revolt led by Li Zicheng of the late Ming period. The new situation created by peasant uprisings during the Ming and Qing indicated that the days of feudalism in China were soon to end.

Friendly intercourse between the Chinese people and the people of other countries began as early as 2,000 years ago when the Han court sent Zhang Qian to the Western Regions, thus opening a road to Central Asia and Persia (present-day Iran). This route over which Han silk fabrics and other products were transported to Southwest Asia and Europe became known in history as the "Silk Road". It promoted economic and cultural exchange between the East and the West. During the Tang Dynasty, with the development of land and sea communications, cultural and trade relations with Korea, Japan, India, Viet Nam, Persia and the Arab countries steadily increased. Emissaries were constantly sent by other countries to the Tang court. Often several thousand foreigners — merchants, students, artists, people of different religious beliefs — were found living in Chang'an, the Tang capital.

Monk Xuan Zang travelled to India and Central Asia and wrote *Da Tang Xi Yu Ji* (*Records of the Western Regions of the Great Tang*), a book of scientific and historical value. Early in the Ming a large fleet under the command of Zheng He made seven long ocean voyages over three decades, sailing to Southeast Asia, the Indian

Peninsula, Persia, several Arab countries and as far as the east coast of Africa. The contacts between China and other parts of the world constantly increased and were interrupted only when the colonialist forces of the West came to the Orient.

In the mid-19th century, the Chinese people of many nationalities who had waged a common fight against their rulers and alien aggressors, turned to fight feudalism and imperialism, and the country entered a new era.

2. MODERN HISTORY (1840-1919)

The Opium War (1840-42)   This war, which was a turning point in Chinese history, marked the beginning of China's gradual transformation into a semi-colonial and semi-feudal society. In fact, the whole history of modern China is one of the Chinese nation fighting against the imperialists and their servants.

In the 17th and 18th centuries the major countries of Europe gradually became capitalist societies. They looked everywhere for markets for their merchandise and seized colonies.

China with its vast territory, rich resources and large population quickly became a target. Early in the 19th century Britain smuggled large quantities of opium into China, leading to grave social and economic consequences. In 1839 the Qing government sent Lin Zexu to Guangdong to ban the use of opium. To protect its opium trade, Britain launched the First Opium War in 1840. While the Chinese people rose spontaneously in armed struggle against the invaders, the corrupt Qing government, fearing for its existence if the people became powerful through fighting the British, preferred to submit to the foreign enemy. In 1842 it signed the "Treaty of Nanking" with Britain, bartering away China's national sovereignty, paying a large indemnity and ceding territory. The United States and France followed Britain's precedent, and compelled the Qing court

"Peking Man".

The site of "Peking Man" dating back 500,000 years.

A 180-mm-high coloured pottery pot of
the Yangshao Culture 6,000 years ago.

A huge vault containing life-size terracotta figurines and horses buried in the tomb of the First Emperor of the Qin Dynasty (259-210 B.C.).

A Tang Dynasty 663-mm-high tricoloured
pottery camel carrying three musicians.

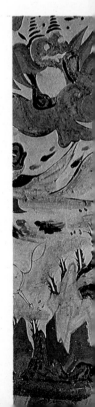

"Flying Celestials and Hunting" — a mural
in No. 249 Cave of the Dunhuang Grottoes,
dating back to the Western Wei (535-56).

The Guyang Cave of the Longmen Grottoes in Henan Province, carved at the end of the 5th century.

The Zhaozhou Bridge in Zhaoxian County, Hebei Province, built in 605-17, is the oldest stone arch bridge still in use today.

The Great Wall — one of the architectural wonders of the world.

Tiananmen (Gate of Heavenly Peace) at
the centre of Beijing, the capital of China.

to conclude similar treaties. These unequal treaties cost China its sovereign rights. The flood of foreign goods into the home market caused the disintegration of its feudal economy. Thus China grew into a semi-colonial, semi-feudal country.

Taiping Revolution (1851-64) After the Opium War the Qing government squeezed the people in every way in order to pay off its huge indemnities. Landlords and rich businessmen shifted the burden of land and business taxes onto the peasants and handicraftsmen and exploited them even more ruthlessly. The working people, no longer able to tolerate such a degree of oppression and exploitation, rose in revolt. Peasant uprisings occurred in many places, finally culminating in the greatest peasant revolutionary movement in Chinese history – the Revolution of the Taiping Heavenly Kingdom.

In 1851 Hong Xiuquan led the peasants in an uprising in Guangxi and established the Tai Ping Tian Guo (Taiping Heavenly Kingdom). With the enthusiastic support of the masses, the Taiping army quickly captured a large part of south China, and in 1853 made Nanjing its capital. The revolutionary forces swept across 17 provinces, captured more than 600 cities and extended their influence far and wide. A land system based on the principle of equal division, called the "Land System of the Heavenly Kingdom", was promulgated, and other measures such as equality of men and women were adopted. Confucian ideas were severely criticized.

As the Qing rule was tottering under the blows of the Taiping forces, Britain and France took the opportunity to start the Second Opium War, wresting by force more privileges from the Qing government. Then Russia joined in. Beside sharing the privileges Britain and France had already obtained, it also seized territory along the Heilongjiang. The foreign powers, in collusion with the Qing court, suppressed the Taiping rebellion, so that in 1864, the Taiping Heavenly Kingdom finally came to an end.

Sino-Japanese War of 1894 The years after the 1870s saw the transition from world capitalism to imperialism, from free competition to monopoly. In the scramble for markets, raw materials and export of capital, the capitalist powers stepped up their invasion of China. In 1884 France launched the Sino-French War against China and Viet Nam. In 1894 Japan started a war against China and Korea — the Sino-Japanese War. Throughout this time, the Qing government, defying popular sentiment, made repeated concessions and compromises and finally concluded the humiliating "Treaty of Shimonoseki" with Japan, whereby Japan received a large part of China's territory, a big indemnity and special privileges in making investments and building factories in certain Chinese ports. This treaty was a heavy shackle on the Chinese people.

After the Sino-Japanese War, the imperialist powers struggled among themselves for investments, leased territories and spheres of influence in China. They tried to carve China up and end its existence as a nation.

For half a century, starting from 1850, tsarist Russia forced China to conclude a series of unequal treaties, extorting many privileges and slicing off a total of 1.5 million square kilometres of China's territory. In this intense rivalry, the United States put forward in September 1899 the so-called "open door" policy, whereby each power's "sphere of influence" in China was recognized, but within these spheres each was not to restrict the trade and navigation of the other powers. Thus, on the one hand, the other powers were to open their spheres of influence to the United States so that its monopoly capital could plunder and exploit the whole of China, and on the other, the sharp contradictions between the imperialist countries were to be mitigated for the time being. A political agreement for the joint partitioning of China was therefore reached among the imperialist powers.

Reform Movement of 1898 In the 1870s Chinese businessmen, landlords and high officials began to invest in modern industrial enterprises. These people later became China's bourgeoisie. Faced with a grave national crisis after the Sino-Japanese War, the bourgeois reformists represented by Kang Youwei and others initiated a movement for political reforms. They advocated constitutional monarchy and the development of agriculture, industry and commerce, hoping to use the emperor's authority to adopt reformist methods to save the nation from extinction and develop capitalism without basically changing the feudal system. They gained the support of a section of the Qing government with Emperor Guangxu at the head, and thus the Reform Movement of 1898 began.

This movement had a certain progressive significance under the historical conditions of the time. It aroused the hostility of the diehards headed by Empress Dowager Cixi, under whose ruthless suppression the Reform Movement quickly and completely failed, with its principal leaders either fleeing or being killed. The failure of this movement proved that bourgeois reformism was absolutely impracticable in semi-colonial, semi-feudal China.

Yi He Tuan Movement of 1900 Confronted by the imperialist partitioning of China, the peasants launched a large-scale anti-imperialist patriotic movement — the Yi He Tuan Movement (known in the West as the Boxer Uprising), which swept the country from 1899 to 1900. In 1900 a joint force of eight imperialist countries — Britain, the United States, Japan, Russia, Germany, France, Austria-Hungary and Italy — invaded China and brutally murdered and looted. The Qing government surrendered to the invaders. Under the combined attack of the counter-revolutionary forces both at home and from abroad, the Yi He Tuan Movement collapsed, but the dauntless struggle of the Chinese people had at least thwarted the imperialists' plan to partition the country.

The Revolution of 1911 After the Yi He Tuan Movement the contradictions between imperialism and the Chinese nation and that between feudalism and the masses of people sharpened. The revolutionary tide in China continued to rise at the beginning of the 20th century. The bourgeois revolutionaries represented by Sun Yat-sen propagated democratic revolution, carrying on an ideological struggle against the reformists and thus enlarging their own camp. To substitute revolution for reformism became an irresistible current of the time. In 1905 the Tong Meng Hui (China Revolutionary League), China's first bourgeois political party, was set up under Sun Yat-sen's leadership. It put forward a programme for bourgeois democratic revolution to "drive out the Tartars, revive the Chinese nation, establish a republic and equalize land ownership". In 1911 the revolutionary groups in Hubei, which had connections with the Tong Meng Hui, persuaded a part of the Qing troops stationed at Wuchang to revolt. Revolutionaries and the masses in other provinces responded, and rebellion quickly spread throughout the country. On New Year's Day, 1912, the Provisional Government of the Republic of China was set up in Nanjing, and Dr. Sun Yat-sen became the provisional president.

The Revolution of 1911 had overthrown the Qing imperial dynasty, founded the Republic of China and put forward a "provisional constitution" for a bourgeois democratic republic. But the feeble Chinese bourgeoisie did not go further to mobilize the people against imperialism and feudalism. On the contrary, it compromised with the counter-revolutionary forces. In February 1912, under the joint attack of the constitutional monarchists who had wormed their way into the revolutionary camp and Yuan Shikai, head of the Northern warlords, Sun Yat-sen, the provisional president, was compelled to resign, and Yuan, the chief representative of the landlord-bureaucrat-comprador class, succeeded to the presidency, stealing the gains of the Revolution of 1911. China then entered a period of rule by the Northern warlords (1912-27).

From the Opium War of 1840, the Chinese people fought for more than 70 years against imperialist and feudal oppression. But their struggles, including the popular revolutionary movements led by Hong Xiuquan and Sun Yat-sen, all failed. History has proved that in semi-colonial, semi-feudal China, neither the peasantry nor the bourgeoisie could lead the revolution to complete victory.

3. CONTEMPORARY HISTORY (1919-49)

May 4th Movement (1919) and the Birth of the Chinese Communist Party (1921) The leadership of the Chinese revolution historically fell upon the rising Chinese proletariat.

China's industrial proletariat was born with the emergence of modern industry. Around 1870, industrial workers in modern China totalled less than 10,000. The number increased to about two million prior to the May 4th Movement in 1919. Though not very numerous, this industrial proletariat represented China's new productive forces and was the most progressive class in modern China.

From the time of its birth the Chinese proletariat continuously fought against oppression and exploitation by foreign capitalism, domestic feudal forces and the bourgeoisie in various ways — political, economic, and otherwise. In 1917, the great October Socialist Revolution broke out in Russia under Lenin's leadership. It inspired China's advanced elements to study and publicize Marxism and the ideas of the Revolution. Consequently a group of intellectuals with incipient communist ideas like Li Dazhao and Chen Duxiu appeared, and these helped to spread Marxism in China. Under the influence of the October Revolution, the May 4th Movement — a great anti-imperialist and anti-feudal revolutionary movement — took place in China, at which the Chinese proletariat demonstrated its might for the first time. Meanwhile Marxism-Leninism spread and linked itself with the revolutionary practice of the Chinese people. In ideology and in training cadres, the May 4th Movement set the stage for the founding of the Communist Party of China. On July 1, 1921, Mao Zedong, Dong Biwu, Chen Tanqiu, He Shuheng, Wang Jinmei, Deng Enming and others, representing the communist groups in different places, met and held the First National Congress in Shanghai to found the Communist Party of China, the vanguard of the Chinese proletariat. Thus the Chinese revolution turned over a new leaf.

Northern Expeditionary War (1926-27) In 1922, the Chinese

Communist Party presented to the Chinese people the first clear-cut programme for a thoroughgoing anti-imperialist and anti-feudal democratic revolution. In 1923, the Party decided to establish a revolutionary united front. It helped Sun Yat-sen reorganize the Kuomintang (the old Tong Meng Hui was reorganized into the Kuomintang after the Revolution of 1911). With the formation of the Kuomintang-Communist united front, the Chinese Communist Party mobilized the masses on a broad scale, and the revolutionary situation developed vigorously. It continued to rise after the death of Sun Yat-sen in 1925. Organized and energized by the Party, the revolutionary forces swept away the reactionary forces in Guangdong, and in 1926 the Northern Expeditionary War began. Supported by the masses, the revolutionary army defeated the counter-revolutionary armies of the Northern warlords and occupied central and south China. The worker-peasant movement grew rapidly throughout the country.

Seeing that the warlord regime they supported was tottering in the sweep of the revolutionary tide, the imperialist forces hastily looked for new agents and finally picked Chiang Kai-shek who had worked his way into the position of "Commander-in-Chief of the National Revolutionary Army". In April 1927, at a crucial moment in the forward advance of the Northern Expeditionary War, Chiang staged, with the active support of the big bourgeoisie and landlord class, a counter-revolutionary coup d'etat against the Chinese Communist Party and the revolutionary people.

Chen Duxiu, General Secretary of the Chinese Communist Party, totally rejected the line represented by Comrade Mao Zedong, and gave up the Party's leadership over the peasantry, the urban petty-bourgeoisie and middle bourgeoisie and in particular the leadership over the armed forces. Chen maintained that in the united front there should be unity in all matters and no struggle. He was afraid that the bourgeoisie would waver in the face of the rising worker and peasant masses. He restricted and opposed armed struggle by the workers and peasants. The result was that when Chiang Kai-shek, representative of the big bourgeoisie and big landlords, betrayed the revolution and massacred the workers and peasants, the masses were left without arms, and the revolution ended in failure.

The Second Revolutionary Civil War (1927-37) The Communists, however, were not intimidated by Chiang's massacres. To save the revolution, an uprising led by Comrades Zhou Enlai, Zhu De and He Long was staged in Nanchang on August 1, 1927. The Nanchang Uprising fired the first shot against the Kuomintang reactionaries.

On August 7, the Central Committee of the Chinese Communist Party held an emergency meeting at which Chen Duxiu was removed from his leading post and his capitulation was criticized and rectified. The meeting established the policy of agrarian revolution and armed uprising. In September, Mao Zedong led the Autumn-Harvest Uprising, organized the first Workers' and Peasants' Red Army and set up the first rural revolutionary base in the Jinggang Mountains on the Jiangxi-Hunan border. In April of the following year, units from the Nanchang Uprising reached the revolutionary base. Led by Mao Zedong, the Red Army repulsed the Kuomintang's three "encircle-ment and suppression" campaigns against the Central Red Base Area, while guerrilla warfare developed in the provinces of Jiangxi, Fujian, Hunan, Hubei, Henan, Anhui, Guangxi, Guangdong, Sichuan and Shaanxi. Mao Zedong made a timely summing-up of their experi-ences, pointing out that in China armed seizure of power could only take the road of establishing rural revolutionary bases, sur-rounding the cities from the countryside and finally capturing the cities.

The Japanese imperialists, anxious to rid themselves of grave political and economic crises, took advantage of Chiang Kai-shek's counter-revolutionary war and the struggles among the new Kuomin-tang warlords to occupy by armed force China's northeastern provinces in 1931, and threaten north China. The country was faced with the crisis of national subjugation. An anti-Japanese movement among the entire people, first of all, among workers, peasants and students, steadily grew. The Chinese Communist Party proposed more than once that civil war should be halted and the country united to resist Japan. The proposals were rejected by Chiang, who, instead, launched even larger "encirclement and suppression" campaigns against the Central Red Base Area in Jiangxi.

At that time Wang Ming, who had assumed leadership of the Party Central Committee, persued his policy of "Left" adventurism, causing great losses to the revolutionary forces: The Red Army soldiers were reduced from 300,000 to 30,000 and Communist Party members from 300,000 to about 40,000. Under these circumstances, the Red Army had to move out. In October 1934, it began its world-famous 25,000-li Long March from Jiangxi.

In January 1935, the Political Bureau of the Chinese Communist Party Central Committee held an enlarged meeting at Zunyi in Guizhou Province. Militarily and organizationally it rectified Wang Ming's "Left" adventurist line and established Mao Zedong's leadership over the whole Party. From then on, the Chinese revolution advanced along a victorious road. In October 1935, the Red Army triumphantly arrived at the Shaanxi-Gansu-Ningxia Border Region. Later it smashed the encirclement campaigns of Chiang Kai-shek. As the Chinese Communist Party fought for the establishment of a national united front against Japanese imperialist aggression, it established its base in the northern Shaanxi city of Yan'an.

The War of Resistance Against Japan (1937-45) On July 7, 1937, the Japanese imperialists perpetrated the Lugouqiao (Marco Polo Bridge) Incident, starting a total offensive against China. Now, with the outbreak of the War of Resistance, there was a unanimous demand among the people for a total war to resist Japanese aggression. The situation forced Chiang Kai-shek temporarily to abandon his traitorous non-resistance policy and take part in the war. But after fighting a few battles, he carried out his policy of actively opposing the Communist Party while passively resisting Japan. He deployed his main forces to encircle and attack the Communist-led popular forces and the anti-Japanese base areas. Consequently, the burden of resistance mainly fell upon the popular forces and the people who opposed Japan. In the last year of the war, the popular forces were holding down 64 per cent of the Japanese troops in China and 95 per cent of their Chinese collaborators' troops.

The Chinese Communist Party led the people in developing production and overcoming difficulties by their own efforts, expanding the people's army and the anti-Japanese base areas and dealing effective blows at the aggressors. At the time of victory over Japan in August 1945, the popular forces had grown to 1.2 million men and the militia over 2,200,000, while the Liberated Areas had a total population of 100 million. The revolutionary strength of the Chinese people grew rapidly.

The Third Revolutionary Civil War (War of Liberation, 1946-49) and the Birth of New China (1949) After the victory over Japan, the people of the whole of China demanded a guarantee of national independence, the abolition of the Kuomintang's one-party dictatorship, the establishment of a democratic coalition government and the implementation of democratic reforms so that China would become independent, free, democratic, united, powerful and prosperous. But Chiang Kai-shek, ever intent on eliminating the Chinese Communist Party, backed by U.S. imperialism, used negotiations as a smokescreen while actively making preparations for a civil war in an attempt to maintain absolute power over the entire nation. To meet the situation, Mao Zedong made plans to counter Chiang's attack while personally going to Chongqing for negotiations to expose Chiang's ruse of saying he wanted peace while actually preparing civil war.

In July 1946, Chiang Kai-shek launched his total offensive against the Liberated Areas. However, with the support of the people in the Liberated Areas and in the Chiang-controlled areas, the Chinese People's Liberation Army, in three years of the War of Liberation, wiped out a total of eight million of Chiang's troops equipped with American arms, and liberated the whole country except for Taiwan Province and a few islands, thus spelling the end of Chiang's rule.

On October 1, 1949, the founding of the People's Republic of China was proclaimed.

Chapter III

POLITICS

1. THE CONSTITUTION OF THE PEOPLE'S REPUBLIC OF CHINA

Four constitutions have been formulated since the establishment of the People's Republic of China. These include the constitution of 1954, the constitution of 1975, the constitution of 1978 and the present Constitution.

The present Constitution was adopted and promulgated for implementation at the Fifth Session of the Fifth National People's Congress held in December 1982. It includes 138 articles in all. Apart from the Preamble, it is divided into the following four chapters: General Principles, the Fundamental Rights and Duties of Citizens, the Structure of the State and the National Flag, the National Emblem and the Capital. The main points are as follows:

Character of the State The People's Republic of China is a socialist state under the people's democratic dictatorship led by the working class and based on the alliance of workers and peasants.

State Power All power in the People's Republic of China belongs to the people. The organs through which the people exercise state power are the National People's Congress and the local people's congresses at different levels. The system of the National People's Congress is China's political system and system of state power.

State Organs The state organs of China include: organs of state power – the National People's Congress and the local people's congresses at different levels; the President of the state; the state administrative organs — the State Council and the local people's governments at different levels; the Central Military Commission of the state; the state judicial organ — the people's courts; the state organ of legal supervision — the people's procuratorates.

The state organs of the People's Republic of China are to apply the principle of democratic centralism.

A Multi-national State   The People's Republic of China is a unified multi-national country. All nationalities in China are equal. The state protects the lawful rights and interests of minority nationalities. Discrimination against or oppression of any nationality are prohibited; any acts that undermine the unity of the nationalities or sow dissension among them are prohibited.

The people of all nationalities have the freedom to use and develop their own spoken and written languages, and to preserve or reform their own customs and ways of living.

Regional autonomy is practised in areas where people of minority nationalities live in compact communities; in these areas organs of self-government are established for the exercise of the right of autonomy.

Economic System   The basis of the socialist economic system of the People's Republic of China is socialist public ownership of the means of production, namely, ownership by the whole people and collective ownership by the working people. The state practises economic planning on the basis of socialist public ownership. It ensures the proportionate and co-ordinated growth of the national economy through overall balancing by economic planning and the supplementary role of regulation by the market.

The individual economy of urban and rural working people, operated within the limits prescribed by law, is a supplement to the socialist economy of public ownership.

The state sector of the economy is the socialist economy under the ownership by the whole people; it is the leading force in the national economy.

Rural people's communes and other forms of urban and rural co-operative economy belong to the sector of socialist economy under collective ownership by the working people. Working people who are members of rural collective economic organizations have the right, within the limits prescribed by law, to farm plots of land and cultivate hills allotted for private use, engage in household sideline production and raise privately-owned livestock.

Socialist public property is inviolable. The state ensures the consolidation and growth of the state economy and protects the lawful rights and interests of urban and rural collective economic organizations and individual economy.

The state permits foreign enterprises, other foreign economic organizations and individual foreigners to invest in China and to enter into various forms of economic co-operation with Chinese enterprises and other economic organizations in accordance with the law of the People's Republic of China.

Fundamental Rights of Citizens   All citizens of the People's Republic of China are equal before the law. The fundemental rights of citizens include:

The right to vote and stand for election;

The freedom of speech, of the press, of assembly, of association, of procession and of demonstration;

The freedom of religious belief;

The freedom of the person, the personal dignity of citizens and the inviolability of their homes;

The freedom and privacy of correspondence which are protected by law;

The right to criticize and make suggestions to any state organ or functionary, and the right to make complaints and charges against, or exposures of, any state organ or functionary for violation of the law or dereliction of duty to relevant state organs;

The right to work, to rest and to receive education, and the freedom to engage in scientific research, literary and artistic creation and other cultural pursuits;

The right to material assistance from the state and society when they are old, ill or disabled;

Women enjoy equal rights with men, and marriage, the family and mother and child are protected by the state; and

The state protects the legitimate rights and interests of Chinese nationals residing abroad and protects the lawful rights and interests of returned overseas Chinese and of the family members of Chinese nationals residing abroad.

Foreign Policy   The People's Republic of China adheres to an independent foreign policy as well as to the five principles of mutual respect for sovereignty and territorial integrity, mutual non-aggression, mutual non-interference in internal affairs, equality and mutual benefit, and peaceful co-existence in developing diplomatic relations and economic and cultural exchanges with other countries. China consistently opposes imperialism, hegemonism and colonialism, works to strengthen unity with the people of other countries, supports oppressed nations and developing countries in their just struggle to win and preserve national independence and develop their national economies, and strives to safeguard world peace and promote the cause of human progress.

2. THE NATIONAL PEOPLE'S CONGRESS

Nature   The National People's Congress of the People's Republic of China is the highest organ of state power. Only the National People's Congress can amend the Constitution, make laws and determines major issues in the country's political life.

Composition   The National People's Congress is composed of deputies elected by the provinces, autonomous regions and municipalities directly under the Central Government, and by the armed forces. The deputies include people from all nationalities, all democratic parties, all people's organizations, all classes and strata. Therefore the National People's Congress is broadly representative.

The composition of the Sixth National People's Congress is as follows:

Deputies	Number	Percentage
Workers and peasants	791	26.6%
Cadres	636	21.4%
Intellectuals	701	23.5%
Democratic parties and patriotic democrats without party affiliation	543	18.2%
People's Liberation Army	267	9.0%
Returned overseas Chinese	40	1.3%
Total	**2,978**	**100%**
Women	632	21.2%
Minority nationalities (each has its own deputies)	403	13.5%

Term The National People's Congress is elected for a term of five years. It meets in session once a year and usually issues announcements and press communiques during the session, publishing relevant documents and information of the session and its results.

Chapter III

The Previous National People's Congresses

Congress	Time*	Place	Number of deputies
First	Sept. 15-28, 1954	Beijing	1,226
Second	April 18-28, 1959	Beijing	1,226
Third	Dec. 21, 1964 - Jan. 4, 1965	Beijing	3,040
Fourth	Jan. 13-17, 1975	Beijing	2,885
Fifth	Feb. 26 - March 5, 1978	Beijing	3,497
Sixth	June 6-21, 1983	Beijing	2,978

*The time listed in the table is the time of the first session.

Functions and Powers

(1) To amend the Constitution;

(2) To supervise the enforcement of the Constitution;

(3) To enact and amend basic statutes concerning criminal offences, civil affairs, the state organs and other matters;

(4) To elect the President and the Vice-President of the People's Republic of China;

(5) To decide on the choice of the Premier of the State Council upon nomination by the President of the People's Republic of China, and to decide on the choice of the Vice-Premiers, State Councillors, Ministers in charge of ministries or commissions and the Auditor-General and the Secretary-General of the State Council upon nomination by the Premier;

(6) To elect the Chairman of the Central Military Commission and, upon nomination by the Chairman, to decide on the choice of all the others on the Central Military Commission;

(7) To elect the President of the Supreme People's Court;

(8) To elect the Procurator-General of the Supreme People's

Procuratorate;

(9) To examine and approve the plan for national economic and social development and the report on its implementation;

(10) To examine and approve the state budget and the report on its implementation;

(11) To alter or annul inappropriate decisions of the Standing Committee of the National People's Congress;

(12) To approve the establishment of provinces, autonomous regions, and municipalities directly under the Central Government;

(13) To decide on the establishment of special administrative regions and the systems to be instituted there;

(14) To decide on questions of war and peace; and

(15) To exercise such other functions and powers as the highest organ of state power should exercise.

The National People's Congress also has the power to recall or remove from office the President and Vice-President of the People's Republic of China; the members of the Standing Committee of the National People's Congress, of the State Council, and of the Central Military Commission; the President of the Supreme People's Court; and the Procurator-General of the Supreme People's Procuratorate.

The NPC Standing Committee   The permanent organ of the National People's Congress is the Standing Committee which is responsible to the National People's Congress and reports on its work to the Congress.

The Standing Committee of the National People's Congress is composed of the Chairman, the Vice-Chairmen, the Secretary-General and other members who are elected on the first session of every National People's Congress. No one on the NPC Standing Committee shall hold any post in any of the administrative, judicial or procuratorial organs of the state. The Chairman and Vice-Chairmen of the Standing Committee shall serve no more than two consecutive terms (five years for each term).

The NPC Standing Committee exercises the following functions and powers:

To interpret the Constitution and supervise its enforcement;

To enact, amend and interpret statutes;

To examine and approve, when the National People's Congress is not in session, partial adjustments to the plan for national economic and social development and to the state budget that prove necessary in the course of their implementation;

To supervise the work of the State Council, the Central Military Commission, the Supreme People's Court and the Supreme People's Procuratorate;

To annul those administrative rules and regulations, decisions or orders of the State Council that contravene the Constitution or the statutes; to annul those local regulations or decisions of the organs of state power of provinces, autonomous regions and municipalities directly under the Central Government that contravene the Constitution, the statutes or the administrative rules and regulations;

To decide, when the National People's Congress is not in session, on the choice of Ministers in charge of ministries or commissions or the Auditor-General and the Secretary-General of the State Council upon nomination by the Premier of the State Council; to decide, upon nomination by the Chairman of the Central Military Commission, on the choice of others on the Commission, when the National People's Congress is not in session.

To appoint and remove Vice-Presidents and judges of the Supreme People's Court and members of its Judicial Committee, and Vice Procurator-General and procurators of the Supreme People's Procuratorate and members of its procuratorial committee;

To decide on the appointment and recall of plenipotentiary representatives abroad;

To decide on the ratification and abrogation of treaties and important agreements concluded with foreign states;

To institute state medals and titles of honour and decide on their conferment;

To decide on the granting of special pardons;

To decide, when the National People's Congress is not in session, on the proclamation of a state of war in the event of an armed attack on the country or in fulfilment of international treaty obligations concerning common defence against aggression; and

To decide on general mobilization or partial mobilization of the whole country.

The Chairman of the NPC Standing Committee presides over the work of the Standing Committee and convenes its meetings. The Vice-Chairmen and the Secretary-General assist in the work of the Chairman. Executive meetings with the participation of the Chairman, Vice-Chairmen and Secretary-General handle the important day-to-day work of the NPC Standing Committee.

NPC Special Committees The National People's Congress establishes a Nationalities Committee, a Law Committee, a Financial and Economic Committee, an Education, Science, Culture and Public Health Committee, a Foreign Affairs Committee, an Overseas Chinese Committee and such other committees as are necessary. These special committees work under the direction of the NPC Standing Committee when the Congress is not in session. The special committees examine, discuss and draw up relevant bills and draft resolutions under the direction of the National People's Congress and its Standing Committee.

3. THE PRESIDENT OF THE STATE

The President and Vice-President of the People's Republic of China are elected by the National People's Congress.

Citizens of the People's Republic of China who have the right to vote and to stand for election and who have reached the age of 45 are eligible for election as President or Vice-President of the People's Republic of China.

The term of office of the President and Vice-President of the People's Republic of China is five years. They shall serve no more than two consecutive terms.

The President of the People's Republic of China shall, as a representative and symbol of the state, exercise the following rights:

To promulgate statutes in pursuance of decisions of the National People's Congress and its Standing Committee;

To appoint and remove the Premier, Vice-Premiers, State Councillors, Ministers in charge of ministries or commissions, and the Auditor-General and the Secretary-General of the State Council;

To confer state medals and titles of honour;

To issue orders of special pardons;

To proclaim martial law;

To proclaim a state of war;

To issue mobilization orders;

To receive foreign diplomatic representatives on behalf of the People's Republic of China;

To appoint and recall plenipotentiary representatives abroad; and

To ratify and abrogate treaties and important agreements concluded with foreign states.

The Vice-President of the People's Republic of China assists in the work of the President. The Vice-President may exercise such parts of the functions and powers of the President as may be deputed by the President. In case the office of the President of the People's Republic of China falls vacant, the Vice-President succeeds to the office of President.

4. THE STATE COUNCIL

The State Council, that is, the Central People's Government, of the People's Republic of China is the executive body of the highest organ of state power as well as the highest organ of state administration. The State Council is responsible, and reports on its work, to the National People's Congress, or, when the National People's Congress is not in session, to its Standing Committee.

Composition The State Council is composed of the following:

Premier;
Vice-Premiers;
State Councillors;
Ministers in charge of ministries;
Ministers in charge of commissions;
Auditor-General; and
Secretary-General.

The Premier has overall responsibility for the State Council and directs its work. The Vice-Premiers and State Councillors assist in the work of the Premier. The term of office of the State Council is five years. The Premier, Vice-Premiers and State Councillors shall serve no more than two consecutive terms.

The plenary meetings of the State Council (composed of all members of the State Council) and executive meetings (composed of the Premier, Vice-Premiers, State Councillors and Secretary-General of the State Council) presided over by the Premier, direct and make policy on important work in various fields within their power.

The State Council has under it 37 ministries and eight commissions. Each ministry has one minister and two to four vice-ministers. Each commission has one minister, two to four vice-ministers and five to ten members. Ministers have the overall responsibility for the ministries and the commissions.

The 37 ministries are:

Ministry of Foreign Affairs
Ministry of National Defence
Ministry of Public Security
Ministry of State Security
Ministry of Civil Affairs

Ministry of Justice
Ministry of Finance
Ministry of Commerce
Ministry of Foreign Economic Relations and Trade
Ministry of Agriculture, Animal Husbandry and Fishery
Ministry of Forestry
Ministry of Water Resources and Electric Power
Ministry of Urban and Rural Construction and Environmental
    Protection
Ministry of Geology and Mineral Resources
Ministry of Metallurgical Industry
Ministry of Machine-Building Industry
Ministry of Nuclear Industry
Ministry of Aeronautics Industry
Ministry of Electronics Industry
Ministry of Ordnance Industry
Ministry of Astronautics Industry
Ministry of Coal Industry
Ministry of Petroleum Industry
Ministry of Chemical Industry
Ministry of Textile Industry
Ministry of Light Industry
Ministry of Railways
Ministry of Communications
Ministry of Posts and Telecommunications
Ministry of Labour and Personnel
Ministry of Culture
Ministry of Radio and Television
Ministry of Education
Ministry of Public Health
Auditing Administration
People's Bank of China
Xinhua News Agency

The eight commissions are:

State Planning Commission

State Economic Commission

State Commission for Restructuring Economic System

State Science and Technology Commission

Commission of Science, Technology and Industry for National
Defence

State Nationalities Affairs Commission

State Physical Culture and Sports Commission

State Family Planning Commission

There are also organs directly under the State Council responsible
for the work in specialized fields:

State Bureau of Goods and Materials

State Bureau of Price Control

State Bureau of Statistics

General Bureau of Industrial and Commercial Administration

General Customs Administration

State Bureau of Meteorology

General Administration of Civil Aviation of China (Civil Aviation
Administration of China)

State Bureau of Oceanography

State Bureau of Seismology

State Bureau of Travel and Tourism

Committee for Reforming the Chinese Written Language

Bureau of Religious Affairs of the State Council

State Archives

Government Offices Administration Bureau of the State Council

Office of Counsellors of the State Council

Office of Overseas Chinese Affairs of the State Council

Functions and Powers The State Council exercises the following
functions and powers:

(1) To adopt administrative measures, enact administrative rules

and regulations and issue decisions and orders in accordance with the Constitution and the statutes;

(2) To submit proposals to the National People's Congress or its Standing Committee;

(3) To lay down the tasks and responsibilities of the ministries and commissions of the State Council, to exercise unified leadership over the work of the ministries and commissions and to direct all other administrative work of a national character that does not fall within the jurisdiction of the ministries and commissions;

(4) To exercise unified leadership over the work of local organs of state administration at different levels throughout the country, and to lay down the detailed division of functions and powers between the Central Government and the organs of state administration of provinces, autonomous regions and municipalities directly under the Central Government;

(5) To draw up and implement the plan for national economic and social development and the state budget;

(6) To direct and administer economic affairs and urban and rural development;

(7) To direct and administer affairs of education, science, culture, public health, physical culture and family planning;

(8) To direct and administer civil affairs, public security, judicial administration, supervision and other related matters;

(9) To conduct foreign affairs and conclude treaties and agreements with foreign states;

(10) To direct and administer the building of national defence;

(11) To direct and administer affairs concerning the nationalities, and to safeguard the equal rights of minority nationalities and the right of autonomy of the national autonomous areas;

(12) To protect the legitimate rights and interests of Chinese nationals residing abroad, and to protect the lawful rights and interests of returned overseas Chinese and of the family members of Chinese nationals residing abroad;

(13) To alter or annul inappropriate orders, directives and regulations issued by the ministries or commissions;

(14) To alter or annul inappropriate decisions and orders issued by local organs of state administration at different levels;

(15) To approve the geographic division of provinces, autonomous regions and municipalities directly under the Central Government, and to approve the establishment and geographic division of autonomous prefectures, counties, autonomous counties and cities;

(16) To decide on the enforcement of martial law in parts of provinces, autonomous regions and municipalities directly under the Central Government;

(17) To examine and decide on the size of administrative organs and, in accordance with the law, to appoint, remove and train administrative officers, appraise their work and reward or punish them; and

(18) To exercise such other functions and powers as the National People's Congress or its Standing Committee may assign it.

5. THE CENTRAL MILITARY COMMISSION

The armed forces of the People's Republic of China belong to the people. Their tasks are to consolidate national defence, resist aggression, defend the motherland, safeguard the people's peaceful labour, participate in the country's construction and endeavour to serve the people.

China establishes the Central Military Commission to direct the armed forces of the country. It is composed of the Chairman, the Vice-Chairmen and members. The term of office of the Central Military Commission is five years.

The Chairman of the Central Military Commission has overall responsibility, and is responsible to the National People's Congress and its Standing Committee.

6. THE LOCAL PEOPLE'S CONGRESSES AND THE LOCAL PEOPLE'S GOVERNMENTS AT DIFFERENT LEVELS

The administrative division of the People's Republic of China is as follows:

a) The whole country is divided into provinces, autonomous regions and municipalities directly under the Central Government;

b) Provinces and autonomous regions are divided into autonomous prefectures, counties, autonomous counties and cities; and

c) Counties and autonomous counties are divided into townships, nationality townships and towns.

Municipalities and major cities are divided into districts and counties. Autonomous prefectures are divided into counties, autonomous counties and cities.

Autonomous regions, autonomous prefectures and autonomous counties are all national autonomous areas.

The state establishes local people's congresses (local people's con-

Administrative Division of the People's Republic of China

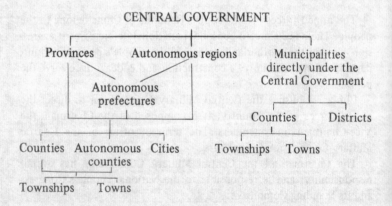

gresses above the county level also establish standing committees) and the local people's governments in the above-metioned administrative areas.

(1) THE LOCAL PEOPLE'S CONGRESSES

Manner of Election Local people's congresses at different levels are local organs of state power. Deputies to the people's congresses of the provinces, autonomous regions, municipalities directly under the Central Government, autonomous prefectures and cities divided into districts are elected by the people's congresses at the next lower level; deputies to the people's congresses of counties, autonomous counties, cities not divided into districts, municipal districts, townships, nationality townships and towns are elected directly by their constituencies.

Term of Office The term of office of the people's congresses of provinces, autonomous regions, municipalities directly under the Central Government, autonomous prefectures and cities divided into districts is five years. The term of office of the people's congresses of counties, autonomous counties, cities not divided into districts, municipal districts, townships, nationality townships and towns is three years.

Functions and Powers Local people's congresses at different levels ensure the observance and implementation of the Constitution, the statutes and the administrative rules and regulations in their respective administrative areas. Within the limits of their authority as prescribed by law, they adopt and issue resolutions and examine and decide on plans for local economic and cultural development and for the development of public services. They elect and decide on the members of the people's governments at their own levels.

Local people's congresses at and above the county level examine and approve the plans for economic and social development and the budgets of their respective administrative areas, and examine and

approve reports on their implementation. They have the power to
alter or annul inappropriate decisions of their own standing committees. They elect and have the power to recall members of the
standing committees, presidents of people's courts and chief procurators of people's procuratorates at the corresponding level.

The Standing Committees of the Local People's Congresses Local
people's congresses at and above the county level establish standing
committees, which are the permanent organs of the people's congresses at the corresponding level and are responsible, and report on
their work, to the people's congresses at the corresponding level. The
standing committee of a local people's congress is composed of a
chairman, vice-chairmen and members elected by the people's congress at the corresponding level.

The standing committees of the local people's congresses at different levels exercise the following functions and powers:

To discuss and decide on major issues in all fields of work in their
respective administrative areas;

To supervise the work of the people's governments, people's
courts and people's procuratorates at the corresponding level;

To annul inappropriate decisions, orders and resolutions of the
people's governments at the corresponding level and at the next
lower level;

To decide on the appointment and removal of functionaries of
state organs at the corresponding level.

The people's congresses and their standing committees of provinces, autonomous regions and municipalities directly under the
Central Government may adopt local regulations which must not
contravene the Constitution, statutes and the administrative rules
and regulations.

(2) THE LOCAL PEOPLE'S GOVERNMENTS

Local people's governments at different levels are the executive bodies of local organs of state power as well as the local organs of state administration at the corresponding level.

Local people's governments at different levels are responsible, and report on their work, to people's congresses at the corresponding level and the state administrative organs at the next higher level, and are under the unified leadership of the State Council. Local people's governments at and above the county level are responsible, and report on their work, to the standing committees of the people's congresses at the corresponding level when the congresses are not in session.

Composition The compositions of the local people's governments of provinces, autonomous regions and municipalities directly under the Central Government are as follows:

Province: governor, vice-governors, secretary-general, department heads, bureau heads and chairmen of committees;

Autonomous region: chairman, vice-chairmen, secretary-general, department heads, bureau heads and chairmen of committees;

Municipality directly under the Central Government: mayor, vice-mayors, secretary-general, bureau heads and chairmen of committees.

The compositions of the local people's governments of autonomous prefectures, counties, autonomous counties, cities, and municipal districts are as follows:

Autonomous prefecture: governor, vice-governors, bureau heads and section heads;

County and autonomous county: county head, vice county heads, bureau heads and section heads;

City: mayor, vice-mayors, bureau heads and section heads;

Municipal district: district head, vice district heads, bureau heads and section heads.

The local people's government of a township or nationality township has township head and vice township heads; the local people's government of a town has town head and vice town heads.

Local people's governments at different levels practise the system of overall responsibility by governors, chairmen, mayors, county heads, district heads, township heads, and town heads.

Functions and Powers Local people's governments at and above the county level have the following functions and powers:

To carry out the resolutions of the people's congresses and their standing committees at the corresponding level, as well as the decisions and orders of the state administrative organs at the higher levels;

To formulate administrative measures, adopt resolutions and issue orders;

To alter or annul inappropriate orders and directives of their subordinate departments and inappropriate resolutions and orders of the people's governments at the lower levels;

To appoint, remove and train administrative functionaries, examine and appraise their work, and reward or punish them;

To implement economic plans and budgets; and

To conduct the administrative work concerning the economy, culture, civil affairs and public security, etc.

The local people's governments of townships, nationality townships and towns carry out the resolutions of the people's congresses at the corresponding level and decisions and orders of state administrative organs at the higher levels, and conduct the administrative work within their own administrative areas.

7. THE PEOPLE'S COURTS AND THE PEOPLE'S PROCURATORATES

(1) THE PEOPLE'S COURTS

Organization The people's courts in the People's Republic of China are the judicial organs of the state. The judicial power of the

People's Republic of China is exercised by the Supreme People's Court, local people's courts at different levels and special people's courts.

The Supreme People's Court is the highest judicial organ. The Supreme People's Court supervises the administration of justice by the local people's courts at different levels and by the special people's courts. The people's courts at higher levels supervise the administration of justice by those at lower levels.

The Supreme People's Court is responsible to the National People's Congress and its Standing Committee. The term of office of the President of the Supreme People's Court is five years, and the President shall serve no more than two consecutive terms.

Local people's courts are divided into three levels: higher people's courts, intermediate people's courts and basic people's courts. Local people's courts are responsible to the organs of state power which created them.

The special people's courts include military courts and other courts.

Task The task of the people's courts is to try cases, both criminal and civil. By judicial process these courts punish all criminals and settle civil disputes so as to safeguard the socialist system, maintain the socialist legel system and public order, protect public property, safeguard the rights and lawful interests of citizens and ensure the development of the socialist revolution and socialist construction.

Some Guidelines The people's courts shall, in accordance with the law, exercise judicial power independently and are not subject to interference by administrative organs, public organizations or individuals.

In judicial proceedings in the courts, the law is applied equally to all citizens, irrespective of their nationality, race, sex, occupation, social origin, religious belief, education, property status, or length of residence. No privileges whatsoever are allowed.

All cases in the courts are heard in public except those involving state secrets, personally shameful secrets and juvenile delinquencies. The accused has the right to defence.

When handling first instance cases, the people's courts adopt the system of the people's assessors who are recommended and elected by the people or by the staff of institutions, people's organizations and enterprises. People's assessors are component members of the courts and have the same power as the judges when they are on duty in the people's courts.

In the administration of justice, the people's courts allow for one appeal to higher court with the decision of the second court being final.

People's courts at all levels establish judicial committees which are the form of organization for the collective leadership of judicial work. Meetings of judicial committees are presided over by the presidents of the people's courts. The task of judicial committees is to sum up the experience gained in trials, and to discuss major or difficult cases as well as other questions concerning judicial work. When there are different opinions during discussions, the principle of majority rule shall be adopted.

(2) THE PEOPLE'S PROCURATORATES

The people's procuratorates of the People's Republic of China are state organs for legal supervision.

The People's Republic of China establishes the Supreme People's Procuratorate and the local people's procuratorates at different levels, in correspondance with the people's courts.

The Supreme People's Procuratorate directs the work of the local people's procuratorates at different levels and of the special people's procuratorates; people's procuratorates at higher levels direct the work of those at lower levels.

The Supreme People's Procuratorate is responsible to the National People's Congress and its Standing Committee. Local people's procuratorates at different levels are responsible to the organs of state power at the corresponding level which created them. The term of office of the Procurator-General of the Supreme People's Procuratorate is five years; the Procurator-General shall serve no more than two consecutive terms.

Functions and Powers   To exercise procuratorial authority over cases of treason and attempts to divide the country, and over major criminal cases of sabotaging the unified implementation of the policies, laws, decrees and administrative orders of the state;

To investigate criminal cases of which the procuratorates themselves have taken direct cognizance;

To examine cases which the public security organs have investigated and make decisions on arrest, prosecution or exemption from prosecution, and to see that the investigatory activities of the public security organs conform to the law;

To institute and sustain prosecution of criminal cases, and to see that the judicial process of the courts conforms to the law;

To see that the execution of judgements and orders in criminal cases and the activities of the prisons, detention houses and establishments in charge of reform-through-labour conform to the law;

The people's procuratorates, in accordance with the law, guarantee the right of citizens to lodge complaints against state functionaries for violating the law and have the legal responsibility to investigate infringements on individual rights, democratic rights and other rights of citizens.

Some Guidelines   In the exercise of procuratorial power by procuratorates at all levels, the law is applied equally to all citizens, and no privileges whatsoever are allowed.

People's procuratorates shall, in accordance with the law, exercise procuratorial power independently and are not subject to interference by administrative organs, public organizations or individuals.

8. POLITICAL PARTIES AND PEOPLE'S ORGANIZATIONS

(1) THE COMMUNIST PARTY OF CHINA

The Communist Party of China was founded on July 1, 1921. It is the vanguard of the Chinese working class, the faithful representative of the interests of the Chinese people of all nationalities, and the core of leadership of the Chinese socialist cause.

The Communist Party of China takes Marxism-Leninism and Mao Zedong Thought as its guiding ideology.

The ultimate aim of the Communist Party of China is the creation of a communist social system. The general task of the Party at the present stage is to unite the people of all nationalities to achieve, in a spirit of self-reliance and hard struggle, the modernization in industry, agriculture, national defence and science and technology and build China into a culturally advanced and highly democratic socialist country.

The Communist Party of China has, over the long experience of revolutionary struggle, formed its own fine style of combining theory with practice, being closely in touch with the masses and exercising criticism and self-criticism.

The Communist Party of China now has over 40 million members. The Communist Party of China is an integral body organized under its programme and Constitution, on the principle of democratic centralism. The Party's leading organizations at all levels are elected by the Party members or their representatives; they shall report on their work regularly to the Party congresses or general membership meetings. They should listen often to the opinions of the masses inside and outside the Party and be subject to their supervision. Party members have the right to criticize or make suggestions to Party organizations and leaders at different levels. They also have the right to bypass the immediate leadership and present their requests, appeals, or complaints to higher Party organizations up to and including the Central Committee. At the same time, all Party activities are under leadership. All Party resolutions are adopted after the Party leading organizations have gathered the opinions of the Party members and the masses. Individual Party members are subordinate to the Party organizations, the minority is subordinate to the majority, the lower Party organizations are subordinate to the higher Party organizations, and all the constituent organizations and members of the Party are subordinate to the National Congress and the Central Committee of the Party. The Party forbids all forms of personality cult. All major issues shall be decided upon by the Party committees after democratic discussion. This is the basic principle of democratic centralism.

The Communist Party of China requires its members to serve the people whole-heartedly, dedicate their whole lives to the realization of communism, and be ready to make any personal sacrifices. The Party members are at all times ordinary members of the working people. Communist Party members must not seek personal gains or privileges, although they are allowed personal benifits and job functions and powers as provided for by the relevant regulations and policies. The Party members must conscientiously observe Party discipline and the laws of the state, take part in the activities of the Party organization and be subject to the supervision of the masses. The Party members must set a good example for the masses at all times in all fields of work and influence and lead the masses forward with their exemplary deeds.

The Communist Party of China has a glorious history of revolutionary struggles. From 1921 to 1949, the Party led the Chinese people in the struggle against imperialism, feudalism and bureaucratic capitalism, winning the victory in the new democratic revolution and establishing the People's Republic of China — a socialist state under the people's democratic dictatorship led by the working class and based on the alliance of workers and peasants. After the founding of the People's Republic of China, the Chinese Communist

Party, as the party in power, has led the Chinese people of all nationalities in safeguarding the state's independence and security, basically completing the socialist transformation of the private ownership of the means of production, conducting planned economic construction on a large scale and achieving unprecedented great developments in China's economic and cultural spheres.

The basic stand of the Communist Party of China in international affairs is: it adheres to proletarian internationalism and firmly unites with the workers of all lands, with the oppressed nations and oppressed peoples and with all peace-loving and justice-holding organizations and personages in the common struggle against imperialism, hegemonism and colonialism and for the defence of world peace and promotion of human progress. It stands for the development of state relations between China and other countries on the basis of the five principles of mutual respect for sovereignty and territorial integrity, mutual non-aggression, mutual non-interference in each other's internal affairs, equality and mutual benefit, and peaceful co-existance. It develops relations with Communist parties and working-class parties in other countries on the basis of Marxism and the principle of independence, complete equality, mutual respect and non-interference in each other's internal affairs.

The highest leading organ of the Communist Party of China is the National Congress of the Party (held every five years) and the Central Committee it creates. The Political Bureau of the Central Committee, its Standing Committee, the Secretariat and the General Secretary of the Central Committee of the Party are elected by the Plenary Session of the Central Committee. The Political Bureau of the Central Committee and its Standing Committee exercise the functions and powers of the Central Committee when the Central Committee is not in session. The Secretariat of the Central Committee attends to the day-to-day work of the Central Committee under the direction of the Political Bureau and its Standing Committee.

The National Congresses of the Communist Party of China

Order	Time	Place	Number of delegates	Party membership
First	July 23-31, 1921	Shanghai	13	over 50
Second	July 16-23, 1922	Shanghai	12	195
Third	June 12-20, 1923	Guangzhou	30	420
Fouth	Jan. 11-22, 1925	Shanghai	20	994
Fifth	April 27 - May 9, 1927	Wuhan	80	over 57,900
Sixth	June 18 - July 11, 1928	Moscow	84 (34)*	over 40,000
Seventh	April 23 - June 11, 1945	Yan'an	547 (208)	1,210,000
Eighth	Sept. 15-27, 1956	Beijing	1,026 (107)	10,730,000
Ninth	April 1-24, 1969	Beijing	1,512	22,000,000
Tenth	Aug. 24-28, 1973	Beijing	1,249	28,000,000
Eleventh	Aug. 12-18, 1977	Beijing	1,510	35,000,000
Twelfth	Sept. 1-11, 1982	Beijing	1,600 (149)	39,000,000

*In brackets are numbers of alternate delegates.

Chapter III

(2) THE DEMOCRATIC PARTIES

These refer to the democratic parties which take part in the patriotic united front led by the Communist Party of China. There are eight of them: the China Revolutionary Committee of the Kuomintang, the China Democratic League, the China Democratic National Construction Association, the China Association for Promoting Democracy, the Chinese Peasants' and Workers' Democratic Party, the China Zhi Gong Dang, the Jiu San Society and the Taiwan Democratic Self-Government League.

These were formed and developed gradually in the period of the anti-imperialist and anti-feudalist new democratic revolution. They had a history of co-operation with the Communist Party in the struggle against imperialist aggression and for people's democracy. From May 1948 to the beginning of 1949, they responded to the Communist Party's call for the convention of the Chinese People's Political Consultative Conference (CPPCC) and, together with the Communist Party and other democratic personages, took part in the First Plenary Session of the CPPCC held in September 1949. It was at this session that the "Common Programme of the CPPCC" was adopted, the Central People's Government organized and the founding of the People's Republic of China proclaimed.

The social basis of these democratic parties was originally the national bourgeoisie, the urban upper-class petty bourgeoisie and their intellectuals, and some other patriots. Now, they have become political alliances for those working people and those patriots supporting socialism with whom they have kept in contact, and political forces which work for socialism.

In its relations with these democratic parties, the Communist Party of China follows the policy of "long-term co-existence and mutual supervision" and "showing utter devotion to each other and sharing honour and disgrace". Within the limits of the rights stipulated by the Constitution of the People's Republic of China, all patriotic democratic parties enjoy full rights of democracy and the freedom to carry out their activities. Since the founding of the People's Republic of China, the democratic parties have conscientiously taken part in consultations on important issues concerning the state, united and encouraged their members and people they associate with to actively take part in all fields of work and practise self-education and self-transformation in their work. A fairly large number of their representative personages are elected deputies to the people's congresses at various levels, and many of their members hold responsible posts in state organs as well as in economic, cultural, educational, scientific and technological departments. The number of democratic party members has seen a major increase. Local organizations and basic organizations of the democratic parties exist in almost all provinces, autonomous regions and municipalities directly under the Central Government and many large and medium-sized cities.

China Revolutionary Committee of the Kuomintang Founded in January 1948, it is mainly composed of patriotic democratic element from the former Kuomintang.

China Democratic League Founded in October 1941, the League was originally called the League of Democratic Political Groups. It took its present name in September 1944. Most of its members are intellectuals in the cultural and educational circles.

China Democratic National Construction Association Founded in December 1945, the Association is mainly composed of formal national industrialists and businessmen, and some intellectuals who are connected with industry and commerce.

China Association for Promoting Democracy Founded in December 1945, its members are mainly intellectuals from cultural, educational (and in particular, teachers of primary and secondary schools) and publishing circles.

Chinese Peasants' and Workers' Democratic Party Originally named the Provisional Action Committee of the Kuomintang founded in 1930, this democratic party changed its name into the Action Committee for Chinese National Liberation in 1935. It adopted its present title in February of 1947. Members are mostly intellectuals from health and medical, cultural and educational circles.

China Zhi Gong Dang It was founded in 1925 by a section of the Hong Men Zhi Gong Tang in America. Its members consist mostly of returned overseas Chinese.

Jiu San Society Founded in 1944 by a group of intellectuals from cultural, educational and scientific circles engaged in the movement for democracy, the Society took as its name the Democracy and Science Forum. On September 3, 1945, in commemoration of the victory in the international war against fascism, it adopted its present name ("Jiu San" means "September the 3rd" in Chinese).

Taiwan Democratic Self-Government League The League was founded in November 1947. Most of its members are patriotic supporters of democracy who originated from Taiwan and now reside on the mainland.

(3) PEOPLE'S ORGANIZATIONS

All-China Federation of Trade Unions This is the supreme leading body of all local federations of trade unions as well as national industrial unions in China.

Following the birth of the Chinese Communist Party in 1921, the Chinese Trade Union Secretariat was founded as the organ for leading the workers' movement. In May 1922, the First All-China Labour Congress was convened in Guangzhou. At the congress, it was recognized that, pending the establishment of the All-China Federation of Trade Unions, the Chinese Trade Union Secretariat was to function as the national liaison centre. The Federation was formally founded at the Second Labour Congress held in Guangzhou in May 1925.

The basic tasks of the All-China Federation of Trade Unions are:

With the socialist modernization as its central work, to mobilize and organize workers and staff members to bring forward innovations in economic organization, system and technology, and to strive to increase production, constantly raising labour productivity, in order to improve the people's material and cultural life;

To resolutely protect the democratic rights of the workers and staff members as masters of the country and their personal interests, while safeguarding the interests of the state and the collective; and

To help the workers and staff members to raise their socialist consciousness, acquire knowledge of science and culture and form a good sense of discipline.

The Communist Youth League of China This is a mass organization of the advanced youth of China. Its basic tasks are:

To educate youth about the spirit of communism and help to arm them with the theory of Marxism-Leninism and Mao Zedong Thought and the knowledge of modern science and culture; and

To help youth to train themselves as successors to the cause of communism with ideals, high morality, good education and strong sense of discipline through their practical experiences in the socialist modernization.

Founded in May 1922, it was first called the Socialist Youth League of China, and renamed the Communist Youth League of China in 1925. In order to unite young people from all walks of life in resistance against Japanese aggression, the Communist Youth League was reorganized in 1937 into the China Youth Association for National Salvation, a much broader mass organization. In April 1949 when nation-wide Liberation was within sight, the Democratic Youth League of China was formed to meet the new situation. It resumed the name of the Communist Youth League of China in 1957.

The Communist Youth League is entrusted by the Chinese Communist Party with the task of guiding the Young Pioneers of China. Founded in October 1949, the latter is a mass organization of

Chinese children.

All-China Women's Federation With women workers, peasants and revolutionary intellectuals making up its main body, the Federation strives to unite women from all walks of life, serving as a bridge to link the Party and Government with the Chinese women. Founded in April 1949 as the All-China Democratic Women's Federation, it adopted its present name in September 1957.

Accounting for half of the country's population, Chinese women are a force not to be ignored. The Chinese Communist Party always attaches great importance to the women's liberation movement. There are women's organizations at all levels, from the national and local, down to the grassroots — which means production brigades in the countryside and neighbourhoods in towns and cities.

The main tasks of women's organizations are:

To conduct ideological education of women on patriotism, communism, women's liberation and equality between men and women;

To encourage women to conscientiously acquire knowledge of culture, science and technology in order to give full play to their ablities in building the socialist modernization;

To protect the legitimate rights and interests of women and children;

To co-ordinate and promote social forces to develop work for children, that is, to promote various educational and welfare undertakings for children; and

To educate women to adopt a correct attitude towards love, marriage and the family and to conduct family planning conscientiously.

All-China Federation of Youth Founded in May 1949 in Beijing, it is a federation of youth organizations in China, with the CYL as its necleus. Originally called the All-China Federation of Democratic Youth, it took its present name in April 1958.

All-China Students' Federation Established in June 1919, it is a federation of student organizations in the universities and colleges throughout the country.

All-China Federation of Industry and Commerce   Founded in October 1953, it originally consisted of industrialists and businessmen throughout the country. Now, it is mostly composed of socialist working people in industry and commerce and patriots who support socialism and the unification of the motherland.

Chinese People's Association for Friendship with Foreign Countries   Founded in 1954 as the Chinese People's Association for Cultural Relations with Foreign Countries, it took its present name in 1969. The Association has as its aim the promotion of mutual understanding and friendship between the Chinese people and other peoples of the world. It seeks to establish contacts with friendly popular organizations and personages in foreign countries, and promotes exchanges between the Chinese and other peoples. All its activities are supported and sponsored by the Chinese Government and people of various circles. At present, it has connections with friendly organizations and personages in more than 130 countries and regions.

9. THE CHINESE PEOPLE'S POLITICAL CONSULTATIVE CONFERENCE

The Chinese People's Political Consultative Conference (CPPCC) is a patriotic united front organization consisting of delegates representing the Chinese Communist Party, the democratic parties, democrats without party affiliation and people's organizations, delegates of all nationalities, people from all walks of life, our compatriots in Taiwan, Hong Kong and Macao and returned overseas Chinese, and specially invited delegates. Guiding itself by the Constitution of the People's Republic of China and its own constitution, the CPPCC holds consultations and offers opinions and suggestions on important issues concerning the country's political life and the patriotic united front.

Following a preparatory meeting in June 1949, the First Plenary Session of the CPPCC was held in Beijing in September of the same year. It exercised the functions and powers of the National People's Congress, adopted the Common Programme of the Chinese People's Political Consultative Conference — provisional constitution — as well as specific laws, organized the Central People's Government and proclaimed the founding of the People's Republic of China. When the First Session of the First National People's Congress was convened in September 1954 and the Constitution of the People's Republic of China proclaimed, the CPPCC ceased to function as the National People's Congress, but continued to exist as an organization of the patriotic united front.

Since the founding of the People's Republic of China, the CPPCC has played an important role in uniting people of all nationalities to oppose internal and foreign enemies, carrying out democratic reform, promoting the socialist transformation, holding consultations on important issues concerning the country's political and economical life, helping democrats in various circles with their ideological transformation, consolidating and developing the patriotic united front, mobilizing all positive factors in the service of socialism, and promoting the international anti-imperialist and anti-colonialist united front.

As China is entering the new historical period with the realization of modernization in industry, agriculture, national defence and science and technology as its central work, the CPPCC's tasks are:

To encourage all the social forces to actively take part in socialist construction;

To unite all the forces that can be united;

To maintain and develop the political situation of stability and unity;

To strive to build China into a modernized socialist country;

To promote the reunification of Taiwan with the mainland; and

To oppose hegemonism and safeguard world peace.

The CPPCC has a national committee and many local committees. The national committee serves a term of five years, and holds a plenary session once a year. The Standing Committee, consisting of a chairman, vice-chairmen, a secretary-general and several members, acts on behalf of the national committee when it is not in session.

Local committees are established according to the administrative division. Organizations of the CPPCC exist in provinces, autonomous regions, municipalities directly under the Central Government, autonomous prefectures, counties, autonomous counties, cities and municipal districts.

The Sessions of the National Committee of the CPPCC

Order	Time*	Place	Number of members (delegates)
First	Sep. 21-30, 1949	Beijing	662
Second	Dec. 21-25, 1954	Beijing	559
Third	April 17-29, 1959	Beijing	1,071
Fourth	Dec. 20, 1964 - Jan. 5, 1965	Beijing	1,199
Fifth	Feb. 24 - March 8, 1978	Beijing	1,988
Sixth	June 4-22, 1983	Beijing	2,039

*It refers to the time of the first meeting of each session.

Chapter IV

ECONOMY

1. AGRICULTURE

(1) BEFORE LIBERATION

China is one of the earliest countries in the world to have engaged in agriculture, a fact archaeologists have established from the traces of a variety of crops and farm tools found at neolithic sites. In the remains of the Hemudu Culture in Zhejiang Province, for instance, large quantities of rice and tools for rice cultivation -- primitive ploughs of bone or wood — were discovered, dating back about 7,000 years. A large quantity of carbonized millet and sorghum grain was unearthed at the sites of Banpo Village (Xi'an) and Dahe Village (Zhengzhou) respectively, both dating back more than 4,000 years. These finds confirm that, as far back as 4,000-7,000 years ago, ancestors of the Chinese had definitely cultivated rice, millet and sorghum in the Yellow River and Yangtze River basins and in the southeastern coastal regions. Historical records clearly indicate that China had from very early years accumulated rich experience in water conservancy and irrigation, making farm implements, cultivation techniques, soil amelioration and the prevention and control of plant diseases and elimination of pests, much of which is still valid in present-day farm work.

However, under feudalism and, in particular, owing to oppression and exploitation under imperialism, feudalism and bureaucrat-capitalism in the last century, little agricultural progress was made before Liberation. There was hardly any advance in agricultural techniques, and productivity remained low.

Formerly 70-80 per cent of the land was in the hands of the landlords and rich peasants who accounted for less than 10 per cent of the rural population while the peasants, who made up more than 90 per cent of the rural population, owned a mere 20-30 per cent of the land. The landless or land-poor peasants were burdened by ruinous rents and taxes. Rent which was paid in kind generally amounted to about half of what they harvested and in some places was as high as 70-80 per cent. Recurrent natural disasters resulting from the destruction of forests and the neglected state of water conservancy works also held down grain output. Other farm and subsidiary production fared no better.

(2) FROM LAND REFORM
TO AGRICULTURAL COLLECTIVIZATION

Immediately after the founding of the People's Republic, land reform was carried out in the countryside under the guidance of the government. This mammoth movement which lasted three years was crowned with success by the end of 1952 when the feudal system of land ownership, which had long held back the development of agriculture, was abolished and about 46 million hectares of land held by the landlords and rich peasants were confiscated and distributed among some 300 million landless or land-poor peasants. After the completion of the reform, the government made efforts to protect and encourage the enthusiasm of individual households for farming while guiding them to take the road of socialist collectivization.

The co-operative movement in China can be said to have progressed in three stages: First the mutual-aid teams, the elementary agricultural producers' co-operatives and then the advanced agricultural producers' co-operatives. From 1951 to early 1953, the government organized the peasants into mutual-aid teams, each consisting of up to a dozen peasant households. The mutual-aid team was a collective labour organization of a rudimentary socialist nature still based on individual household plots. Following the December 1953 Party Central Committee Resolution on the Development of Agricultural Co-operatives, the mutual-aid teams were turned into elementary agricultural producers' co-operatives of a semi-socialist nature, characterized by the pooling of land as shares under unified management. Mao Zedong's report "On the Co-operative Transformation of Agriculture" in July 1955 was followed by the adoption of the Resolution on the Co-operative Transformation of Agriculture at the Sixth Plenary Session of the Seventh Party Central Committee held in October the same year. Both of these were published as documents and clearly defined the policies and principles regarding agricultural co-operation, the specific steps, and the methods of exercising leadership over the co-ops, thereby expediting the advent of the high tide in agricultural co-operation. By the end of 1956, over 96 per cent of all peasant households had joined agricultural producers' co-operatives, among which 87.8 per cent were in advanced co-ops of a socialist nature. In the advanced agricultural producers' co-ops, no remuneration was given for the land pooled, the co-op members' draught animals and farm implements were owned collectively after the original owners were paid in cash, and the principle of distribution according to work was applied. By then, the socialist transformation of private ownership of the small-scale peasant economy into collective ownership had in the main been completed in China's rural areas.

By the end of 1958, all the agricultural producers' co-ops throughout the country had changed over to communes. In 1982, there were more than 54,000 people's communes and 2,000-odd state farms in China.

The people's commune was both a state organization of political power at the grass-roots level and an organization of collective economy. Since the system of "integrating government administration with commune management" was proved by practice not suitable to the needs of the developing situation in the countryside, the state decided in 1982 to establish township governments, with people's communes still existing as organizations of collective economy. This task is presently being carried out throughout the country.

(3) THE DEVELOPMENT OF AGRICULTURE

Since the founding of the People's Republic of China, the state has attached great importance to agricultural development. The credit funds allocated to the rural areas amounted to 224.1 billion yuan from 1952 to 1981.

At present, there are more than 66,000 small hydro-electric power stations which are linked to the national grid, and almost all the people's communes and more than half of the production brigades are provided with electricity. In 1983, the power consumption in rural areas amounted to 43.52 billion kwh., 871 times that of 1952. Many villages today use electricity for water lifting, the processing of farm and sideline products and home lighting.

Big advances have also been made in water conservancy, as by 1983 China had built 87,000 large, medium and small reservoirs. The acreage under irrigation increased to 44.64 million hectares, which is 2.3 times that of 1952. In a number of provinces and autonomous regions, the irrigated acreage accounts for half their total cultivated area. Two-thirds of the low-lying land are now no longer prone to waterlogging, and half of the alkaline land has been leached.

Northern and southern China are frequently subject to drought or waterlogging, and this leads to unstable yields. To remedy this kind of situation, the state has made great efforts to tame the Yellow

River, Huaihe River, Haihe River and other more unruly rivers. Dykes have been constructed or reinforced along the major rivers, and more than 100 big man-made waterways for draining flood-waters and excessive rainfall have been built. The acreage of crop-land giving high and stable yields despite drought or excessive rainfall is growing rapidly.

In 1983, China had 840,000 large and medium tractors which ploughed 40 per cent of the country's arable land. The irrigation and drainage machines amounted to 78.49 million h.p. and the power of agricultural machinery totalled 245 million h.p., 149 times that of 1957. Mechanization in sowing, hoeing, harvesting and trans-port is also developing rapidly.

However, manual labour still predominates in agricultural produc-tion. This is due to the country's vast area, with huge numbers of people tilling a proportionally small amount of land under a great diversity of natural and production conditions and employing assorted farming methods. Agricultural mechanization has to be car-ried out step by step and by taking into account the varying condi-tions in different places.

Agro-scientific research institutes set up by the central and local authorities have helped to spread more scientific farming practices. In addition to comprehensive research institutes, there are specializ-ed institutes for research studies in grain, cotton, tea, fruit trees, vegetables, tobacco, bee-keeping, tussah silkworm raising, bast-fibre plants, forestry, aquatic products and meteorology. Stations for popularizing better agricultural techniques, veterinary centres and seed stations have been established at the county, district and commune levels. A nationwide agro-scientific and technical network has taken shape. Many new achievements have been made, and much experience has been gained over the last few years in selecting fine seed strains, preventing and controlling plant diseases, eliminating pests and improving cultivation techniques and soil.

To develop agriculture, the government adopted a series of

significant policies and measures in 1978: raising the purchasing price of farm produce, respecting the decision-making power of production teams and commune members, restoring private plots and rural fair trade, abolishing unnecessary restrictions on household sidelines and establishing all forms of the production responsibility system. All of these, especially the responsibility system, have enabled a better implementation of the socialist principle of distribution of "to each according to his work" and stimulated the peasants' enthusiasm for production.

According to the fixed price of 1980, the total output value of agriculture in 1982 reached 262.9 billion yuan, 4.55 times that of 1949. (The value rose by an average annual rate of 4.7 per cent while it was only 2.7 per cent in Japan, 2.5 per cent in the Soviet Union, 1.9 per cent in Britain and 1.8 per cent in West Germany from 1949 to 1979.)

Since the founding of the People's Republic of China, the output of some major farm produce has increased greatly. In 1983, the output of grain was 387.28 million tons, 3.42 times that of 1949; cotton 4.637 million tons and edible oil 10.55 million tons.

The great achievements in agriculture have not only helped industry, but also solved the problem of food and clothing for the more than 1 billion people with a per capita area of cultivation at only 0.1 hectare. To readjust the agricultural structure, grain was imported over the years, but accounted for only 3 to 4 per cent of China's total grain output each year.

(4) FOOD AND CASH CROPS

Food Crops The sown acreage of food crops accounts for about 79.2 per cent of the total cropland in 1983. Distribution of crops varies significantly over different parts of the country, because of social, historical and natural conditions. Generally speaking, the southern areas are major paddy-rice producers while the northern

The Output of Major Farm Produce (1949-83)

Item	Unit	1949	1952	1978	1982	1983
Grain	1,000 tons	113,200	163,900	304,750	353,430	387,280
Cotton	1,000 tons	445	1,304	2,167	3,598	4,637
Peanuts	1,000 tons	1,268	2,316	2,377	3,916	3,951
Rape-seed	1,000 tons	734	932	1,868	5,656	4,287
Sesame	1,000 tons	326	481	322	342	349
Jute and bluish dog-bane	1,000 tons	37	306	1,088	1,060	1,019
Tea	1,000 tons	41	83	268	397	268
Silk-worm cocoon	1,000 tons	31	62	173	271	401
Sugar cane	1,000 tons	2,642	7,116	21,117	36,882	31,141
Beat	1,000 tons	191	479	2,702	6,712	9,182
Aquatic products	1,000 tons	450	1,670	4,660	5,155	5,460
Draught animal (year-end number)	1,000 heads	60,020	76,460	93,890	101,130	103,500
Pig (year-end number)	1,000 heads	57,750	89,770	301,290	300,780	298,540

and western areas grow mainly wheat, maize, barley, millet and potatoes. In northeast China, after maize, wheat and soya bean, sorghum is the main crop. Maize is dominant on the plains and in the hilly areas of northern China.

China is one of the major rice producers in the world. In 1982 paddy made up 29 per cent of the total acreage sown to food crops and 46 per cent of the total grain output.

As most parts of China lie within the East Asian monsoon zone, the natural conditions such as sunshine, temperature and moisture favour the cultivation of paddy-rice. However, rice cultivation is no longer confined to the Yangtze River valley and areas south of it; it is now being successfully grown even as far as the northern part of Heilongjiang Province, and much dryland has been converted into paddy-fields.

China is one of the earliest countries to have cultivated wheat, and the current sown acreage and wheat output are next only to paddy-rice.

Wheat is quite hardy and can endure cold and drought relatively well. This makes it possible to grow wheat in many areas in the north and south and on the plains and plateaus. The wheat-growing areas north of the Qinling Mountains and the Huaihe River account for about one half of the national wheat acreage. Henan Province leads the country in wheat output, followed by Shandong and Hebei. The wheat grown in these three provinces is mainly winter wheat. Colder areas north of the Great Wall and west of the Minshan and Daxue mountains including Inner Mongolia Autonomous Region, Heilongjiang, Jilin and Qinghai provinces are major spring wheat producers.

High-yielding maize is planted widely on the plains and in the mountainous and hilly areas from Heilongjiang Province to the Yunnan-Guizhou Plateau. China is next only to the United States in the production of maize.

Soya bean originated in China and is an important food and

oil-bearing crop. The Songliao Plain in the northeast is China's biggest marketable soya bean base. In 1982, it made up only 37.8 per cent of the nation's total soya bean acreage but produced 43.2 per cent of the national total. Soya bean from northeast China is known in the international market for its fine quality.

Cash Crops There is a great variety of cash crops grown in all parts of China. Among them are traditional export items such as bast fibres, tung oil, silk and tea.

Cotton is China's most important raw material in the textile industry and takes up one-third of the total acreage for cash crops. China today is one of the leading cotton growers in the world. There are essentially two major cotton-growing areas in China. One is in the north which encompasses the North China Plain, the Fenhe-Weihe river valley and the basins north and south of the Tianshan. The other area is in the south and contains the Middle-Lower Yangtze River Plain and the Sichuan Basin. Both the quantity and quality of cotton have been raised considerably since Liberation as a result of popularizing fine strains and the prevention and control of plant diseases and of pests.

Bast-fibre cultivation has a long history in China. Prior to the 15th century, garments in China were chiefly of bast fibres and silk. China grows ambary hemp, ramie, flax, hemp and jute. Jute is grown widely in provinces and regions south of the Yangtze River, particularly in the Pearl River Delta and Hangzhou Bay. Ambary hemp is grown on the plain bordering the Bohai Sea. China is the home of ramie and the world's biggest producer. Hubei, Hunan, Jiangxi and Sichuan provinces are the major growers. Flax is grown mainly in Heilongjiang and Jilin provinces in the northeast.

Silk has long been a famous product of China. Before the turn of the 20th century, China topped the world in silk production. But sericulture was on the decline before Liberation because of intrusion by external forces which ruined the industry, and backward production methods. After Liberation, however, it recovered rapidly.

Silkworms are now raised in more than 20 provinces and autonomous regions. The area around the Taihu Lake, the Pearl River Delta and the Sichuan Basin are the three major sericultural centres.

Oil-bearing crops include soya bean, peanut, rapeseed, sesame and linseed. China is an important world producer of peanut. The crop is mainly grown on the Shandong Peninsula, the Yellow River-Huaihe River Plain and the hilly areas in the southeast. Shandong Province alone produces more than one quarter of the nation's total. China leads the world in rapeseed, which is mainly produced on the Middle-Lower Yangtze River Plain and the Sichuan Basin. Sesame is China's special product from the plain north of the Huaihe River and areas on the middle and lower reaches of the Hanjiang River. In addition, cotton seed, castor bean, tea oil camellia and walnut are also important oil-bearing plants in China.

Sugar cane and sugar beet are the major sugar-bearing crops. The former is grown in the southern provinces of Guangdong, Taiwan, Fujian, Sichuan and Yunnan, and the Guangxi Zhuang Autonomous Region. The latter is grown in Heilongjiang and Jilin provinces and the Inner Mongolia Autonomous Region in the north where the climate is cool and there are long hours of sunshine.

China was the first country to discover the tea plant and cultivate it for its leaves. Its large variety of tea falls under two main categories — green tea and black tea — depending on the method of preparation. The big tea groves are mostly in the Yangtze River valley and in the provinces and regions to the south of the valley. Some of the world-famous Chinese teas are Hangzhou's Longjing tea, Anhui black tea, Yunnan black tea and Yunnan green tea. Chinese tea is a favourite drink in many parts of the world.

The variety of fruit in China is tremendous, and much of it finds a ready international market. The main fruits include pears, apples, oranges, tangerines, peaches, apricots, plums, green plums, persimmons, grapes, jujubes, loquats, longans and lichees, of which the latter four are Chinese specialities. The Liaodong and Shandong

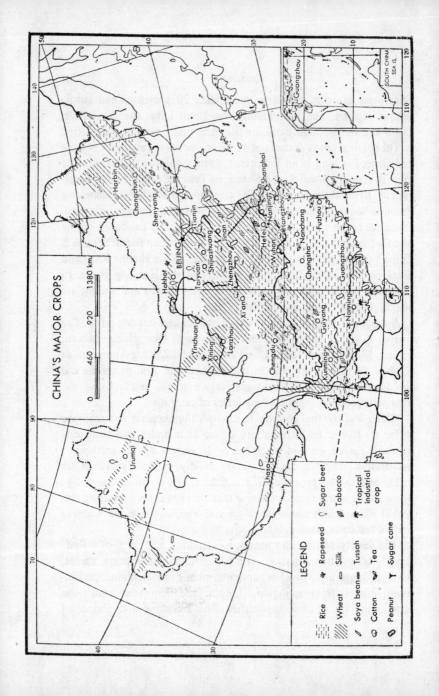

CHINA'S MAJOR CROPS

LEGEND

Rice
Wheat
Soya bean
Cotton
Peanut

Rapeseed
Silk
Tussah
Tea
Sugar cane

Sugar beet
Tobacco
Tropical industrial crop

0   460   920   1380 km

SOUTH CHINA SEA IS.

peninsulas are famous areas producing temperate fruits, and apple output in the southern part of Liaoning Province is the largest in the country. The Turpan Basin in the Xinjiang Uygur Autonomous Region is known for its fine large white grapes. The southern provinces abound in oranges and tangerines. Guangdong and Fujian are noted for their tropical and subtropical fruits such as bananas, lichees, longans and pineapples.

(5) FORESTRY, ANIMAL HUSBANDRY AND FISHERY

Forestry There are four major afforested areas in China, namely, the northeast, the north and northwest, the southwest, and the south. The first has the largest afforested area and is the biggest source of timber. The undulating Greater Hinggan Mountains have the largest conifer acreage. There are larches, Scotch pines and birches. The Lesser Hinggan Mountains and the Changbai Mountains are known for their dense woods of Korean pine and larch. The dense forests are inhabited by a large variety of fauna including the rare northeast China tiger, sable, otter, lynx and sika deer.

Southwest China, especially the northwestern part of the Yunnan-Guizhou Plateau and the southeastern part of the Qinghai-Tibet Plateau, is another region of natural forests. There are dense groves of spruce, fir, teak, mahogany and camphor. Xishuangbanna in southern Yunnan Province is considered a natural botanical garden. More than 5,000 species of trees are found there. It is also a sanctuary for 62 species of tropical animals and some 400 species of tropical birds. Its precious animals and birds include the Asian elephant, bison, gibbon and peacock.

Forest reserves are relatively few in north and northwest China. In the north, they are found mainly in the Luya and Luliang mountains in Shanxi Province and the Yanshan Mountains in Hebei Province. In the northwest, there are forests on the northern slopes of the Tianshan and the southern slopes of the Altay, in areas north of the Qilian Mountains, on the Qinling, along the Bailong River and on the Weibei Plateau. The major species include the Chinese pine, oak, fir, spruce and birch.

South China, with its warm, humid climate, is a tropical and subtropical forest base with a great variety of trees, including the spruce and horse-tail pine. There are also the oil tea camellia, tung oil tree, lacquer tree and bamboo, all of great economic value. Camphor, rubber, oil palm, coconut, cinnamon, coffee and cinchona are grown in Guangdong, Taiwan and Fujian provinces and the Guangxi Zhuang Autonomous Region.

In order to protect the fauna and flora and to carry out scientific research, China has designated many natural preservation zones, among which, the Changbai Mountains in Jilin Province, the Wolong reserve in Sichuan Province and Dinghu Lake in Guangdong Province are chosen as international natural preservation zones.

Since Liberation, a nationwide movement has been launched to cover the country with trees. Statistics show that by the end of 1976, 28 million hectares of land had been afforested. This, together with the original forest cover, brings the afforested acreage to 120 million hectares. The average afforested area in recent years reached more than 4 million hectares each year. The tree-covered areas have expanded to 12.5 per cent of the total land area. However, China's afforested acreage is below the average world level and ranks 120th in the world. To protect the existing forests and expedite the work of afforestation, China promulgated in 1979 a Forest Law.

Animal Husbandry Good conditions exist for developing animal husbandry, for the country has 320 million hectares of grasslands. China's most important livestock-breeding bases include Heilongjiang, Inner Mongolia, Ningxia, Xinjiang, Gansu, Qinghai and Tibet where the minority peoples of the Mongolian, Tibetan, Kazak, Kirgiz, Tajik and Yugur nationalities who live in compact communities are mostly engaged in livestock breeding. Sheep are the most important domestic animals, followed by cattle and horses.

After Liberation, many herdsmen moved into settlements instead of leading nomadic lives. Grass has been sown in a number of areas, and fodder bases have been set up. At the same time veterinary, artificial insemination and fine-stock stations have been established and fine strains bred and popularized in pastoral areas.

The Hulun Buir and Ujimqin grasslands on the Inner Mongolia Plateau which produce a rich cover of grass are good natural grazing grounds for such draught animals as the famous Ujimqin horse, Sanhe horse and Sanhe ox. On the broad grassland in Xilin Gol graze the famous Mongolian sheep.

Natural highland pastures are located mostly around the Tarim and Junggar basins and on the mountain slopes and valleys of Xinjiang. This areas is an important producer of fine stock. Among the fine strains of animals raised in the Ili River valley are the Ili horse and fine-wool sheep.

In central, east and south China where agriculture is dominant, animal husbandry is an important subsidiary activity. In farming areas, pigs are the chief animals besides sheep, goats and draught animals such as oxen, horses, donkeys and mules. Poultry are also widely raised in China.

Fishery After Liberation, with the establishment of state-owned aquatic products companies and marine fishing companies in Shanghai, Qingdao, Tianjin, Liaoning, Hebei, Zhejiang, Jiangsu and Fujian and the introduction of more and better fishing vessels, output has gone up several times, and that of 1983 reached 5.46 million tons. New fishing techniques are also being adopted on an increasingly extensive scale.

There are some 1,500 species of marine fish in Chinese waters, mostly of the warm-water type, such as the hairtail, yellow croaker, herring, cuttlefish, jellyfish and prawn.

Along the coast are four major fishing areas, in the Bohai Sea, the Yellow Sea, and the East China and South China seas. There are famous fishing grounds just off the Zhoushan Islands, the Miaodao

Islands between the Shandong and Liaodong peninsulas, the Chang-shan Islands, Taiwan, coastal Fujian, Guangdong and Guangxi and the South China Sea islands. Dalian, Yantai, Qingdao, Shanghai, Guangzhou and Beihai are important fishing bases complete with refrigeration facilities and plants for processing fish meal and cod-liver oil and a variety of other fish products. In addition, there are more than 667,000 hectares of shallow seas for cultivating shellfish, kelp and laver.

China has a total fresh-water surface of 16 million hectares, of which 5 million hectares are suitable for pisciculture and the cultiva-tion of aquatic products. Among the more than 700 species of fresh-water fish are some 50 of economic value such as the black carp, Chinese ide, silver carp, big-head carp, common carp and crucian carp. The last two are extensively distributed because they are highly adaptable and prolific. The first four are special Chinese fish. Furthermore, there are salmon in the Wusuli River and the Heilongjiang River, shad in the Yangtze River and Xijiang River and white-bait in the lower reaches of the Yangtze River, all well-known and popular.

2. INDUSTRY

(1) OUTLINE

Before 1949 industry played a very small role in China's back-ward national economy. Factories were ill-equipped and the level of technology was very low. The industries were unevenly developed and distributed. Light industry, mainly the textile and food indus-tries, accounted for upwards of 70 per cent of the total value of industrial output. Heavy industry contributed very little and the machine-building industry accounted for only 1.7 per cent of the total value of industrial output. Industry was concentrated mainly along the eastern seaboard. Most of the iron and steel, machine-building, electricity generating, textile and basic chemical industries were located in Shanghai, Tianjin, Qingdao, Shenyang, Anshan and a few other cities. There was almost no modern industry in the vast interior.

Immediately after Liberation, all enterprises of a bureaucrat-capitalist nature were confiscated and turned into state-owned socialist enterprises. Capitalist industry and commerce began to be gradually transformed along socialist lines through state-private ownership. Individual handicraft industries were also collectivized.

By 1956 the socialist transformation of agriculture, handicrafts and private industry and commerce from private to public or collective ownership was basically completed, and the means of production were put under public ownership. These changes in the relations of production were a powerful stimulus to the development of the productive forces.

After the founding of the People's Republic, three years were spent on restoring the war-torn national economy. This was accomplished by 1952, when the total value of industrial output was higher than the highest pre-war level. The development of the national economy was started in 1953 in a planned way. The investment in industrial capital construction totalled 464.4 billion yuan from 1952 to 1982. A huge number of large and medium-sized industrial projects have been completed or extended, new industries, new products, new technologies and new processes have emerged. A fairly comprehensive industrial system has been established.

The distribution of the industries changed markedly. Not only were the original industrial enterprises along the coast fully utilized and rationally developed, but new industrial bases and industrial centres were built in the vast hinterland.

The present problems in China's industry are: the imbalance in the development between industry and agriculture, the irrational inner structure of industry, the low level of technology and management, and low economic results. In view of this situation, China, in 1979, decided on an economic policy of readjustment, reform, consolidation and improvement, which has shown remarkable success.

The Output of Major Industrial Products

Item	Unit	1949	1952	1978	1982	1983
Raw coal	million tons	32	66	618	666	715
Crude oil	million tons	0.12	0.44	104.05	102.12	106.07
Electricity	billion kwh	4.3	7.3	256.6	327.7	351.4
Pig iron	million tons	0.25	1.93	34.79	35.51	37.38
Steel	million tons	0.158	1.35	31.78	37.16	40.02
Timber	million cubic metres	5.67	11.20	51.62	50.41	52.32
Cement	million tons	0.66	2.86	65.24	95.20	108.25
Chemical fertilizer*	million tons	0.006	0.039	8.693	12.78	13.73
Farm pesticide	thousand tons	–	2	533	457	331
Power generating equipment	thousand kw	–	6	4,838	1,645	2,740

Item	Unit	1949	1952	1978	1982	1983
Machine tools	thousand	1.6	13.7	187	100	121
Automobile	thousand	–	–	149	196	240
Tractors	thousand	–	–	113.5	40	37
Walking tractors	thousand	–	–	324.2	298	498
Chemical fibre	thousand tons	–	–	284.6	517	541
Yarn**	thousand tons	327	656	2,382	3,354	3,270
Cloth**	billion metres	1.89	3.83	11.03	15.35	14.88
Machine-made paper & cardboard	thousand tons	110	370	4,390	5,890	6,610
Sugar	thousand tons	200	450	2,270	3,384	3,770
Crude salt	million tons	2.99	4.95	19.53	16.38	16.13
Cigarettes	million boxes	1.60	2.65	11.82	18.85	19.38
TV sets	million	–	–	0.5173	5.92	6.84
Bicycles	million	0.014	0.08	8.54	24.20	27.58
Sewing machines	million	–	0.066	4.865	12.86	10.87
Watches	million	–	–	13.51	33.01	34.69

*Chemical fertilizer is calculated as 100% effective.
**Yarn and cloth include blend fabrics.

(2) IRON AND STEEL, NON-FERROUS AND
MACHINE-BUILDING INDUSTRIES

Iron and Steel Industry Immense and sustained efforts have been made over the past 30 years and more to build up the iron and steel industry. Steel production in 1949 was only 158,000 tons. By 1983 it had leapt to 40.02 million tons, with more than 1,000 types of steel products. With domestically produced steel, the country has built ocean freighters, supersonic aircraft and satellites with its own steel.

After 1949, the then existing iron and steel works were reconstructed and expanded, many new works were established and the location and distribution of the industry was improved and rationalized. Anshan, Shanghai, Beijing, Wuhan, Benxi, Baotou, Ma'anshan and Chongqing are now all important iron and steel bases.

Anshan, China's largest iron and steel base, mines its own ores and makes its own iron and steel, rolls its own steel and has plants which produce various iron and steel products. In the substrata in and around Anshan is one of the few large deposits of iron-ore in the world. To its north about 100 kilometres away is Fushun, China's "coal capital". To its east is the big Benxi coal-field. Not far to the south is the Dashiqiao magnesium mine which, as China's biggest, provides refractory materials for the iron and steel works in Anshan.

The iron and steel base of Benxi is famous for its high-grade iron. Communications here are good, and the rich iron ore, limestone, coking coal and other major raw materials necessary to the industry are easily accessible. In addition, the iron ore in the Nanfen area in Benxi has an extremely low phosphorus content and produces a special high-quality steel used in shipbuilding and electrical motors industries.

A new and developing iron and steel base is to be found in Wuhan at the point where the Beijing-Guangzhou railway trunk line and the

Level fields on the Middle-Lower Yangtze River Plain.

Transplanting rice.

Wheat harvest on the North China Plain.

Ripening Sorghum on the Northeast Plain.

A threshing-ground in the Taihang Mountain area.

Harvesting kenaf in Laixi County, Shandong Province.

Tea picking.

An orange grove.

A greenhouse in Yuyuantan Commune, suburban Beijing.

Stand of Korean pines in the Lesser Hinggan Mountains.

In Inner Mongolia.

Shrimp catch.

Daqing Oilfield in northeast China.

Rolling mill of the Anshan Iron and Steel Complex, northeast China.

Datong, Shanxi Province, a major coal base.

The Liujiaxia Hydro-electric Power Plant.

A synthetic ammonia plant in Sichuan Province.

Inside the Shanghai No. 9 Textile Mill.

The famous blue-white and colour glazed porcelain ware of Jingdezhen, Jiangxi Province.

The 6,772-metre-long rail and road Yangtze
River Bridge at Nanjing, completed in 1969.

A section of the 902-kilometre-long Hunan-Guizhou Railway.

The Sichuan-Tibet Highway.

Shanghai Harbour, China's biggest port.

Bambooware of south China on display at the twice-a-year Guangzhou Export Commodities Fair.

Yangtze River meet. Communications by land and water are convenient. Close by is the Daye iron mine. Rich deposits of iron ore lie under the surrounding hills.

Since the Wuhan Iron and Steel Complex went into operation in 1958, it has expanded continuously and now has iron-smelting plants, iron-ore mines, and steel-making plants, as well as sintering plants, coking plants, rolling mills and other ancillary works. A big rolling mill was established here in 1978. With equipment from West Germany, Japan and some other countries, it turns out various kinds of hot- and cold-rolled sheet steel.

Shanghai, China's largest comprehensive industrial city at the mouth of the Yangtze River, leads the country in the industrial technology and the production of rolled steel products of many varieties. To enable Shanghai to expand its iron and steel industry the Meishan Iron-Ore Mine in Anhui has been completed and will become one of the main suppliers of ore to Shanghai.

Panzhihua, located on the banks of the Jinsha River in Sichuan Province, is one of the steel bases in China. With rich local vanadium-titanium-magnetite ore, it produces high-grade alloy steel.

Non-ferrous Metallurgical Industry Many provinces and autonomous regions of China such as Liaoning, Jilin, Shanxi, Inner Mongolia, Gansu, Hubei, Hunan, Jiangxi, Yunnan, Guizhou, Guangdong, Guangxi and Anhui have rich non-ferrous metal resources. Dayu in southern Jiangxi has the world's largest tungsten mine. Xinhua in central Hunan is the world's largest producer of antimony. Gejiu in Yunan is known as the "tin centre" and produces about three-quarters of the country's tin. The cinnabar from the mine in Tongren Prefecture in eastern Guizhou Province is world-famous. The copper mines of Dongchuan in Yunnan, Gaolan in Gansu and Tongling in Anhui are also very well known, as are the zinc and lead mines of Shuikoushan in Hunan and the bauxite of Shandong and Hunan.

Long ago the Chinese people learnt to extract non-ferrous ores from the earth and to smelt them. In the Bronze Age, an amalgam of copper and tin was used to mint coins, weapons and utensils. However, before Liberation, the extraction and smelting of non-ferrous ores was never properly developed and the domestic demand for non-ferrous materials was almost entirely met by imports.

Since the founding of the People's Republic, every province and autonomous region have set up their own mining and metallurgical works. Non-ferrous metal products have greatly improved in quality and increased in quantity. All the 60 or so non-ferrous metals used in the world are being smelted in China. Besides meeting domestic requirements, some are exported.

Shenyang and Shanghai are the largest non-ferrous metallurgical centres.

Machine-building Industry This industry turns out products to equip industries such as the metallurgical and mining, electricity-generating, petroleum, chemical, light and textile, automotive, tractor, machine-tool, instrument and meter, locomotive and rolling-stock, aeroplane and shipbuilding.

The geographical distribution of the machine-building industry has changed remarkably. The original machine-building enterprises located along the coast have been greatly expanded, so that Shanghai, Tianjin, and Shenyang are now important machine-building bases, while many new machine-building centres have been set up in the interior. Even in Tibet, which formerly had no industry at all, there are now machine-building plants.

Tremendous efforts are being put into the development of the agricultural machinery industry to boost agricultural production. Most provinces, autonomous regions and municipalities have their own tractor or walking-tractor plants. With the exception of a few counties in Tibet and Xinjiang, all counties today have their own workshops making and repairing farm machinery. The better-known tractor centres are Luoyang, Tianjin, Changchun, Anshan, Shanghai and Nanchang.

Progress has also been made in the locomotive and rolling-stock industry. Before Liberation, China was only able to repair locomotives. But now, the steam, diesel and electric locomotives running on the lines, as well as passenger coaches and goods waggons are all made in China.

(3) FUEL AND POWER INDUSTRIES

Coal Industry. China's coal resources are mostly concentrated in the northern part of the country. The coal-rich Shanxi Province has a reputation as the "Home of Coal".

China was the first country to discover and use coal. Coal was reported to have been found in 200 B.C., in what is now the vicinity of Nanchang in Jiangxi Province. By the seventh century, coal was already in use for smelting ores. However, before Liberation the rich coal resources were never rationally exploited. There were only a few coalmines, and all were poorly equipped and technically backward. A little more than 30 million tons were produced annually before China began the swift development of its coal industry after Liberation. In 1957, its production had risen to 130 million tons. Annual output since 1978 has always maintained a level of more than 600 million tons, next only to the United States and Soviet Union, ranking third in the world.

The coal industry was formerly concentrated in Liaoning, Shanxi and Hebei provinces, with very little coal mined elsewhere. After Liberation, a great number of large and medium-sized shafts were built in the country. Coal has been found and is being extracted even in Tibet. In the southern provinces such as Jiangsu, Zhejiang, Anhui, Jiangxi, Fujian, Hubei, Hunan, Guangdong and Guangxi, coal output has risen steeply.

North China produces the largest amount of coal, followed by the northeast and then central-south and east China. Kailuan, Datong, Yangquan, Huainan, Shizuishan, Xuzhou, Huaibei and Baoding are all important coal bases in China.

The Kailuan Mines in Tangshan, Hebei Province, supplies one of the best types of coal for the power and chemical industries. To its east is the port city of Qinhuangdao, outlet for coal from the Kailuan Mines. The mines were badly damaged in the severe earthquake of July 1976 in the Tangshan-Fengnan area but production was restored quickly, and the annual output reached more than 20 million tons.

Datong Mines in northern Shanxi Province near the Yanmenguan Pass cover an area of about 2,000 square kilometres. The coal is of excellent quality and can be used as power fuel without washing. There are 16 pairs of huge shafts operating today, and their output in 1982 was 26 million tons, ranking first in the country.

However, the coal industry is still a weak sector in China's national economy and needs to be built up considerably. The work to upgrade the coal bases in Shanxi Province and Inner Mongolia Autonomous Region is being accelerated.

Oil Industry Before Liberation, no serious explorations for oil were made. In the years between 1904 and 1948, total production amounted to about 2 million tons. Foreign companies monopolized the oil market in China. The building of the Yumen, Karamay and Qaidam oilfields in the 50s was followed by the Daqing Oilfield, built in the early 60s. Thus China began to produce enough oil to meet its own needs.

The Daqing Oilfield in the Songnen Plain of northeast China has been expanded continuously, and from 1976 to 1983 the annual output had been maintained at a level of above 50 million tons.

The construction of Daqing was followed by the building of the Shengli, Huabei (including Dagang and Renqiu), Nanyang and Liaohe oilfields.

The Renqiu Oilfield is located in the Central Hebei Plain, where, for the first time, oil was discovered in China in the strata of the Sinian System. This led to the development of the "Buried Hill", or

Guqianshan geological concept. Exploratory drilling began in 1975, and in the following year some high-yield wells were discovered.

The successive discovery of new oilfields has altered the geography of China's oil industry. Now there is the Daqing Oilfield in the northeast, the Huabei oilfields in the north, the Shengli Oilfield in the east, the Yumen, Karamay and Qaidam oilfields in the northwest, and the natural gas fields of Sichuan in the southwest.

Offshore explorations for oil have started and experimental drilling has begun in some places.

In 1978-83, China produced more than 100 million tons of crude oil annually, ranking sixth in the world.

In order not to overtax the railways as oil production rose rapidly, China laid its first oil pipeline in 1974, starting from Daqing and ending at the important Bohai port of Qinhuangdao. This 1,152-kilometre pipeline was extended from Qinhuangdao to Beijing the following year. In 1978, the oil pipeline from Linyi in Shandong Province to Nanjing was completed. This system carries crude oil from the Daqing, Shengli, Liaohe and Huabei oilfields to refineries and ports.

Refineries have developed swiftly in step with the immense increases in crude oil production. Since 1960, old refineries have been reconstructed and expanded and many new ones set up. In this period, refining capacity doubled and redoubled. In addition to the refineries in the new oilfields of Daqing, Shengli and Dagang, Beijing, Lanzhou, Fushun, Dalian, Jinxi, Shanghai, Tianjin, Nanjing, Chongqing and Guangzhou have also built oil-refining facilities.

Currently, some 640 specifications of oil are being produced. China is now an important oil-producing country with an independent and fairly complete oil industry of its own.

Power Industry China is richly endowed with coal and hydro-power resources and their geographical distribution is extremely favourable. Coal dominates in the north, and hydro-power resources in the southwest. These are favourable conditions for developing

China's electric power industry.

Power Industry developed very slowly before Liberation. In the 67 years from 1882, when the first power plant was built in Shanghai by a British company, to 1949, the whole country's electricity-generating capacity was only 1.9 million kw., and its annual output was 4,300 million kwh.

Since Liberation, a number of large and medium-sized power plants have been built. In the whole country, there are 2,800-odd power stations, each with a generating capacity of over 500 kw., among which 74 are large thermal power plants and hydro-electric stations, each with an installed capacity of over 0.25 million kw. In 1983, the country produced 351.4 billion kwh. of electricity, 82 times that of 1949. A number of large power grids have been set up, so that there are now 20 grids, each with a capacity of over 500,000 kw., among which, each of the 12 grids has an installed capacity of over 1 million kw.

China's largest hydro-electric power plant is the Liujiaxia Hydro-electric Power Plant built across a deep ravine of the Yellow River on the western outskirts of Lanzhou in Gansu Province. The ravine here is only 60 metres wide and the flow is swift. The main dam, 147 metres long astride the river, produces a head of 100 metres. The plant has five sets of generators with a total installed capacity of 1,225,000 kw. With an annual output of 5,700 million kwh., which is more than that in the whole of China before Liberation.

Lower down the river from Liujiaxia, other big and medium-sized hydro-power plants have been built at Yanguoxia, Bapanxia, Qingtongxia, Sanshenggong and Sanmenxia, together with water control projects.

The Yangtze River, with a drop of more than 5,000 metres from its source to its estuary, is a rich source of hydro-electric power. Before Liberation, there were only a few small power stations along its entire length. Today, large and medium-sized hydro-electric power plants along its course number over two dozen. The Danjiangkou Plant in Hubei, the Zhexi Plant in Hunan, the Yilihe Plant in Yunnan, and the Longxihe Plant in Sichuan are all well-known water power projects on its tributaries.

The local authorities have also built large numbers of small hydro-electric power plants by themselves.

A further series of hydro-electric power plants on the Yangtze, Yellow, Hanshui, Dadu and Wujiang rivers are envisaged to tap China's rich water resources to meet the needs of the country's economic growth. Work is already under way on the power plants at Gezhouba on the Yangtze River, at Longyangxia on the upper reaches of the Yellow River, and at Wujiangdu on the Wujiang River in Guizhou Province.

Research work on nuclear energy, geothermal energy, methane and solar energy is being carried out and these energy resources are also being used.

(4) CHEMICAL INDUSTRY

China's chemical industry has three main branches: basic chemicals, chemical fertilizers and organic synthesis. The cities of Nanjing and Dalian are the two biggest producers of industrial sulphuric acid. Large sulphuric acid plants have been built in the chemical fertilizer and other industrial bases.

Shanghai and the provinces of Liaoning, Jilin and Sichuan are the chief producers of nitric acid, while hydro-chloric acid is produced mainly in the cities of Tianjin and Shanghai. The soda ash and caustic soda industries were established before Liberation. Soda ash is produced in the big coastal cities and the inland salt-producing areas of Sichuan, Qinghai and Inner Mongolia. Caustic soda is produced widely, chiefly in Dalian, Tianjin, Shanghai, Shenyang, Taiyuan and Chongqing.

The chemical fertilizer industry is one of the fastest expanding industries. In pre-Liberation days, there were only two chemical fertilizer plants in Dalian and Nanjing and the production was low. In 1971-75, China imported 13 sets of large chemical fertilizer installations, which were all completed and went into operation in 1979. Today, all municipalities, provinces and autonomous regions have their own fairly large chemical fertilizer producing centres.

More nitrogenous fertilizer is produced than any other chemical fertilizer. The largest nitrogenous fertilizer producer is the Daqing Chemical Fertilizer Plant in Heilongjiang Province built in June 1976. Other large plants are being operated in Jilin, Taiyuan, Shijiazhuang, Shanghai, Kaifeng, Wuhan, Zhuzhou, Guangzhou, Lanzhou, and Shandong. Nanjing and Taiyuan are the biggest phosphatic fertilizer producers in China. In addition, a great number of small chemical fertilizer plants were also set up all over the country, producing half of the country's output of nitrogenous fertilizer.

The organic synthesis chemical industry was set up after the founding of the People's Republic. It uses coal, petroleum and natural gas as raw materials and turns out plastics, synthetic rubber, synthetic dyestuffs, medical and paint products, and ethylene. Shanghai is the biggest organic synthesis industrial base, followed by Jilin, Beijing, Tianjin, Taiyuan and Lanzhou.

(5) LIGHT INDUSTRY

Textile Industry This is not only the most important branch of the country's light industry, but also a key sector in the economy as a whole. It produces cotton, wool, silk, flax, chemical fibre and knit goods. In 1982, its total output value was 9.3 times that of 1952, providing enough clothing for the 1 billion people.

The cotton textile industry is the biggest of the entire textile industry. In 1982, the output of cotton yarn was 10 times that of 1950. The distribution of the textile industry has been made more rational. New cotton-growing areas have been set up in the vicinity of the existing cotton-spinning centres such as Shanghai, Tianjin,

Qingdao and Wuxi. At the same time, new cotton-spinning enterprises were established near the cotton-producing areas inland. Examples are Beijing, Handan, Shijiazhuang, Zhengzhou, Xi'an, Wuhan and Urumqi.

As early as 4,000 years ago, the Chinese people were already weaving and wearing silk. By the second century, silk began to be exported. But from the beginning of the 20th century the domestic silk industry was almost ruined. Fortunately, it made a rapid and remarkable recovery after 1949. In 1982, the nation's raw silk production went up 18.3-fold, compared with 1950. China ranks first in the world in quantity of silk exported, and her silk fabrics have regained their reputation for fine quality.

The silk filatures are located mainly in the silk-producing Yangtze River and Pearl River deltas and the Sichuan Basin. Shanghai, Hangzhou, Suzhou, Wuxi, Chongqing, Chengdu, Huzhou and Nanjing are all very famous for silk production. Dandong and Fengcheng on the Liaodong Peninsula and Qingdao, Yantai and Zhoucun on the Shandong Peninsula are China's tussah silk centres.

The Chinese linen industry can be broadly divided into three parts: the making of gunnysacks, ramie textiles and flax fabrics. After Liberation, the old gunnysack industry expanded, and large new plants were established recently in Hangzhou, Guangzhou, Chengde and Tianshui.

Ramie spinning also goes back to an early date in Chinese history and its product — grass linen — enjoys a well-earned reputation throughout the world. Since Liberation, grass linen production has been mechanized in the chief producing centres of Yichun and Wanzai in Jiangxi, Liuyang and Liling in Hunan and Longchang in Sichuan. Several modern plants have been built near ramie-growing areas.

The flax fibre industry is a new one. It was established only after the country's Liberation, but it has already outstripped ramie production. The biggest flax fibre centre is Harbin in Heilongjiang.

Wool spinning and weaving has been advancing rapidly, and the distribution of the industry is being rationalized. Some plants have been moved out of Shanghai to the northwest, and many new ones established in areas inhabited by minority nationalities where animal husbandry is more developed. The wool centres include Lanzhou, Xining, Xianyang, Yinchuan, Hailar, Baotou, Hohhot, Urumqi, Hotian, Kashi and Lhasa.

In recent years, the chemical fibre industry has made swift headway. Main chemical fibre industry centres include Shanghai, Beijing, Nanjing, Dandong, Baoding, Xinxiang, Changzhou, Qingdao, Shijiazhuang and Xiangfan.

Foodstuffs, Paper-making and Ceramics An infinite variety of foodstuffs are produced in China. Flour, rice milling, distillery and cooking oil industries operate in towns and cities across the country. Sugar and dairy product enterprises have been built close to raw material sources. Taiwan is the country's biggest cane sugar producer, but the industry has also been making headway in Guangdong, Sichuan and Fujian provinces and the Guangxi Zhuang Autonomous Region. Heilongjiang Province in the northeast is the biggest beet sugar producing base.

China abounds in salt deposits. Salterns dot its long coast starting from the Liaodong Peninsula in the north to Hainan Island in the south. The Changlu Saltern at Bohai Bay and the Huaibei Saltern in Jiangsu Province are the best-known. In addition, enormous quantities of lake, well and rock salt are produced in the interior. The city of Zigong in the Sichuan Basin, for example, is the oldest and best-known producer of well salt. Lake salt is found in many places in northwest China and in the Inner Mongolia Autonomous Region.

China was the first country in the world to make paper. Besides writing, packing, and other common types of paper, there are special papers for various industrial and agricultural uses. Shanghai is one of the older paper-making centres while the paper-making industry in

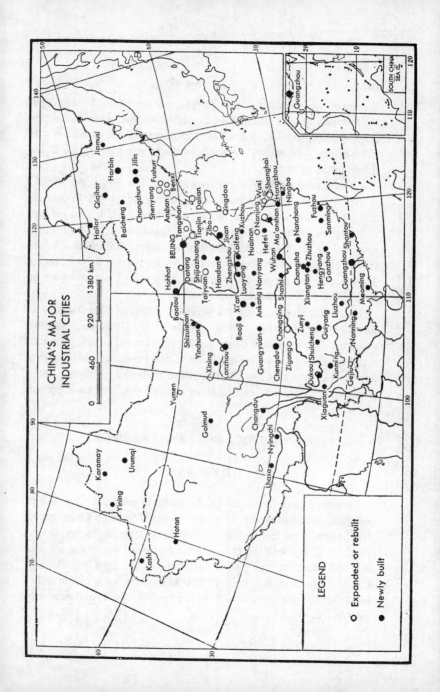

CHINA'S MAJOR
INDUSTRIAL CITIES

LEGEND

○ Expanded or rebuilt

● Newly built

the northeast is relatively new. Large quantities of hand-made paper are turned out in a number of provinces in the south. Non-wood pulp — reeds, bagasse, rice, wheat and cotton stalks, as well as wild fibre plants — is occupying an increasingly important place in the manufacture of paper.

Chinese ceramics have a very long history. The very name "china" is synonymous with porcelain. The ancient industry is flourishing and developing today. The world-famous blue-white, *fen cai* and colour glazed wares of Jingdezhen in Jiangxi Province, the fine china from Liling in Hunan and Tangshan in Hebei, the prized celadons from Longquan in Zhejiang, the dark brown pottery from Yixing in Jiangsu and the carved pottery from Foshan in Guangdong are all well received on the world market.

China has also built up many new branches of light industry to meet popular demands and the needs of the developing national economy. These include those making plastics and plastic products, watches, bicycles, sewing-machines, cameras, household electrical appliances, optical glass, photosensitive materials, synthetic detergents, synthetic perfumes, etc. Many of these products are exported.

3. COMMUNICATIONS AND TRANSPORT

(1) RAILWAYS

Prior to Liberation, most of the railways were built by foreign concerns, and during the 73 years from 1876, when China got its first railway, to 1949, only 22,000 kilometres of railways were constructed. Much of the network was destroyed during the national and civil wars in this period, so that by the time the People's Republic was founded, only 11,000 kilometres were usable. Since then, most of the lines have been repaired or rebuilt and new ones constructed.

In the southwest there was previously no trunk line, except a narrow-gauge railway in Yunnan Province, so that communication with the provinces further inland was almost cut off. After 1952, a number of major railways were built, including the Chengdu-Chongqing, Baoji-Chengdu, Guizhou-Guangxi (Guiyang-Liuzhou), Sichuan-Guizhou (Chongqing-Guiyang), Guiyang-Kunming, Chengdu-Kunming and Hunan-Guizhou (Zhuzhou-Guiyang) railways, thus facilitating access to the rest of the country.

Northwest China was virtually inaccessible before Liberation. At that time, the Longhai Railway (from Lianyungang in Jiangsu to Lanzhou in Gansu) only reached as far as Tianshui in Gansu, while the section from Baoji to Tianshui, owing to poor engineering, was often inoperable. With the completion of the Tianshui-Lanzhou Railway in 1952, the whole Longhai line was open to traffic. The 1,892-kilometre Lanzhou-Xinjiang Railway, built in 1962, snakes westwards from Lanzhou and passes through the mountains of the Tianshan Range before it finally reaches Urumqi, seat of the Xinjiang Uygur Autonomous Region. From there through-trains are available to Beijing or Shanghai.

Another trunk line in the northwest is the Baotou-Lanzhou Railway which links the vast northwest of the country with Inner Mongolia. Its eastern terminus connects with the Beijing-Baotou Railway and the western terminus with the Lanzhou-Xinjiang, the Lanzhou-Qinghai and the Longhai lines, thus linking together Baotou (an iron and steel centre), the Hetao and Yinchuan plains (rich cotton and grain areas) and Lanzhou (a large industrial city).

To date, more than 100 new lines have been constructed, amounting to 51,600 kilometres, excluding the large mileage of double-tracking, forest lines and lines for other special uses scattered all over the country. With the exception of Tibet, every province, municipality and autonomous region on the mainland is now reached by railway. The lines in southwest and northwest China account for 25 per cent of the nation's entire network. To further ease the access of the frontier areas to the inland provinces, new railways are being built. The Hairag-Golmud Section (in Qinghai Province) of the 2,049-kilometre Qinghai-Tibet Railway has been constructed and commissioned.

Efforts are being made for the electrification of China's railway network. In addition to the electrified Baoji-Chengdu, Yangping-guan-Ankang (in Shaanxi) lines, and Shijiazhuang-Taiyuan multiple-track line which has been eletrified since 1982, another four are under construction.

The number of rail bridges has grown. In the old days there was not a single bridge over the Yangtze River, while over the Yellow and Qiantang rivers there were only three rail bridges, built by foreign contractors. Since Liberation, 13 rail bridges and over 20 highway bridges have been built over the Yellow River and four railway bridges over the Yangtze River. The Chinese-designed and built Yangtze River Bridge at Nanjing, completed in January 1969, is a double-decker (motor road above and railway beneath) with a span of 6,772 metres, making it the longest in this country.

New Trunk Lines

Name	Between	Year Open to Traffic	Length (km.)
Chengdu-Chongqing	Chengdu-Chongqing	1952	505
Tianshui-Lanzhou	Tianshui-Lanzhou	1952	348
Lanzhou-Xinjiang	Lanzhou-Urumqi	1962	1,904
Hunan-Guangxi	Hengyang-Pingxiang	1952	1,011
Baoji-Chengdu	Baoji-Chengdu	1956	671

Baotou-Lanzhou	Baotou-Lanzhou	1958	990
Yingtan-Xiamen	Yingtan-Xiamen	1956	694
Lanzhou-Qinghai	Lanzhou-Haiyan	1960	313
Sichuan-Guizhou	Chongqing-Guiyang	1965	424
Guiyang-Kunming	Guiyang-Kunming	1966	635
Chengdu-Kunming	Chengdu-Kunming	1970	1,099
Hunan-Guizhou	Zhuzhou-Guiyang	1972	902
Jiaozuo-Zhicheng	Jiaozuo-Zhicheng	1970	753
Xiangfan-Chongqing	Xiangfan-Chongqing	1978	840
Zhicheng-Liuzhou	Zhicheng-Liuzhou	1978	885
Beijing-Tongliao	Beijing-Tongliao	1979	870
Anhui-Jiangxi	Wuhu-Guixi	1981	551
South Xinjiang	Turpan-Korla	1981	476

(2) HIGHWAYS

According to 1983 statistics, the total road network open to traffic was 910,000 km., 11 times that in 1949.

The highway to Tibet is a most formidable project in highway construction. The Tibet Autonomous Region, located on the Qinghai-Tibet Plateau (the "Roof of the World"), previously did not have a single highway and the chief means of transport were horses and yaks. Now three principal highways — the Sichuan-Tibet (Chengdu-Lhasa), Qinghai-Tibet (Xining-Lhasa) and Xinjiang-Tibet (Yecheng-Burang) highways — have been built.

The Sichuan-Tibet Highway, 2,413 kilometres in length, starts from Chengdu in the east and ends at Lhasa in the west. From the Chengdu Plain up to the Tibet Plateau, it winds across the Hengduan mountain range and descends to the Lhasa River valley, passing through Ya'an, Kangding, Garze and Qamdo. Along the way are high mountains and deep ravines, the relative difference between the two extremes reaching as much as 2,000 metres in some places. The road crosses over such swift rivers as the Dadu, the Jinsha, the Lancang and the Nujiang, and the Erlang, Chola and Nyainqentanglha mountains. A reinforced concrete highway bridge now spans the Nujiang River, where previously a bamboo-chain bridge hung precariously between the towering cliffs above the river.

The Qinghai-Tibet Highway starts westwards from Xining, climbs Riyue Mountain, winds along the southern bank of the Qinghai Lake, through the Qaidam Basin and up to the new industrial town of Golmud in Qinghai Province. It then turns southwards, climbs the Kunlun Mountains, over the Qinghai-Tibet Plateau and finally reaches Lhasa by joining the Sichuan-Tibet Highway in Nagqu. Half of its total length of 1,965 kilometres stands more than 4,000 metres above sea level on a frozen plateau where the air is thin.

The Xinjiang-Tibet Highway along China's western frontier, starting from Yecheng (Kargilik) in southern Xinjiang, runs southwards to Burang in western Tibet. It is 1,455 kilometres long with an average elevation of 4,200 metres and is the highest road in the world.

A number of highways in the mountainous inland provinces have been built where communication used to be particularly poor. More than 90 per cent of rural communes are accessible by road.

(3) INLAND NAVIGATION

China has a large number of rivers whose total navigable length exceeds 400,000 kilometres. Of this, 108,900 kilometres were open to navigation in 1983.

With 80,000 kilometres in service, the Yangtze River is the longest and busiest river in China. The section from Yibin down to the coast is navigable to steamboats all the year round, while the section between Shanghai and Wuhan can take 10,000-ton ships in the highwater season. The Yangtze River valley is rich in natural resources and along its course are some of China's major industrial cities, such as Chengdu, Chongqing, Wuhan, Nanjing and Shanghai.

Large-scale work has been done in dredging the river and improving navigation aids. The "Three Gorges", the section east of Yibin known for its treacherous rapids, is now navigable day and night.

The Yangtze River has many ports, the main ones being Chongqing, Yichang, Zhicheng, Shashi, Wuhan, Huangshi, Jiujiang, Anqing, Wuhu, Ma'anshan, Nanjing, Zhenjiang, Nantong and Shanghai.

Chongqing is the biggest port on the upper reaches of the Yangtze River where the Jialing River joins it. The Chuanjiang River links Chongqing with the major cities on the lower and upper reaches of the Yangtze River. Sailing north from Chongqing along the Jialing one can reach Guangyuan County in northern Sichuan and sailing south along the Wujiang River one can reach the northwestern part of Guizhou Province. All three rivers are minor sections of the Yangtze River.

At the confluence of the Yangtze and Hanshui rivers is Wuhan, one of the country's biggest inland ports. Handling freight mainly of coal, ores and iron and steel, Wuhan ranks second only to Nanjing among the ports along the main stream of the Yangtze River in its annual transport volume. About 140 kilometres east from Wuhan is Huangshi. Built after Liberation, it is a principal port on the middle reaches. These two large ports are connected by rail.

Another port on the south bank of the Yangtze River is Wuhu, which is linked to Nanjing, Ma'anshan and Tongling by rail. The port, at the confluence of the Yangtze and Qingyi rivers, is an important clearing-house for rice and the economic centre of south Anhui Province. Opposite Wuhu on the north bank of the Yangtze River is Yuxikou, the outlet for coal from the Huainan and Huaibei coal fields which combine to form the biggest coal supplier in east China. This port is only a little more than 100 kilometres southeast from Hefei, the capital of Anhui Province.

Nanjing is on the intersection of the Beijing-Shanghai and Nanjing-Wuhu railways. With deep and wide waters, the Nanjing Harbour can berth 10,000-ton ships all the year round. The port of Nanjing handles mainly coal, petroleum, ores, building materials, chemical fertilizer and iron and steel. It is a major land and water transport junction in the lower Yangtze River valley and the most important port along the main stream of the Yangtze River in its total transport volume.

The Pearl River flows through sub-tropical China where there is heavy rainfall. Carrying an enormous flow of water, it is formed by the confluence of three rivers — the Xijiang, Beijiang and Dongjiang — and has a total length of 12,000 kilometres (including trunk and tributaries) open to navigation. Boats can reach Nanning, the capital of Guangxi, and its industrial centre of Liuzhou. The Xijiang, its main stream, takes up 80 per cent of the total transport volume of the entire river system.

Other navigable rivers include the Heilongjiang, Huaihe, Haihe and Minjiang.

The Grand Canal is also an important waterway. It stretches 1,800 kilometres from Beijing's Tongxian County southwards to Hangzhou in Zhejiang Province. In the past, because of poor maintenance, only a short section of it was navigable. Dredging has extended its all-season navigable length to 1,000 kilometres.

(4) MARINE TRANSPORT

Along the coast are many fine harbours. The coastal transport system is divided into two zones – the northern and the southern. The former, with Shanghai as its chief port, covers the following main shipping lines:

Shanghai – Qingdao – Dalian
Shanghai – Qingdao – Tianjin
Shanghai – Qinhuangdao
Shanghai – Lianyungang
Shanghai – Ningbo
Shanghai – Wenzhou
Dalian – Weihai
Dalian – Tianjin
Dalian – Qinhuangdao – Lianyungang

The southern zone, with Guangzhou as its centre, includes the following main lines:

Guangzhou – Zhanjiang
Guangzhou –Shantou
Guangzhou – Beihai
Guangzhou – Dongfang (Basuo)

China has established a marine fleet consisting of bulk freighters, tankers, passenger liners and container ships. Chinese ships visit more than 400 ports in over 100 countries and regions.

China operates four main marine navigation routes starting from Shanghai, Tianjin, Guangzhou, Dalian and Qingdao:

Eastern route: to Japan and to Canada, the United States and Latin American countries.

Western route: across the Indian Ocean, through the Suez, the Mediterranean into the Atlantic Ocean, or rounding the Cape of Good Hope to the Atlantic, calling at ports in South Asia, West Asia,

Africa and Europe.

Southern route: to countries of Southeast Asia and Oceania.

Northern route: to Korea and the ports on the east coast of the Soviet Union.

The major harbours on the mainland are Dalian, Qinhuangdao, Tianjin, Yantai, Qingdao, Lianyungang, Shanghai, Ningbo, Fuzhou, Xiamen, Huangpu and Zhanjiang.

Tianjin, the gate to Beijing from the sea, consists of the three harbours of Neigang, Tanggu and Xingang. Xingang at the mouth of the Haihe River is the biggest man-made harbour to be built after Liberation.

Shanghai Harbour is the biggest in China. The Huangpu River connects its docks to the urban districts. Shanghai serves the Yangtze River and Huaihe River valleys and the southeast coastal areas. It is also China's largest industrial city. Therefore the port leads in the volume of flow of goods in inland navigation and in foreign trade.

Dalian Harbour on the southern tip of the Liaodong Peninsula is deep, wide and ice-free. It is the biggest trading port in the northeast, handling most of northeast China's industrial and agricultural products which go by sea. Dalian's new oil harbour completed in 1976 has oil pipes direct from the Daqing Oilfield.

Huangpu Harbour is a natural outlet of the Pearl River drainage system. It serves all the southern provinces and is the most important port along the southeast coast. Its geographical location is advantageous as regards trade with Southeast Asia and Europe.

Much work has been done in building new docks and expanding old ones. Starting in 1972, 42 deepwater berths for ships of 10,000 tons have so far been built at Dalian, Qinhuangdao, Tianjin, Yantai, Qingdao, Lianyungang, Shanghai, Huangpu and Zhanjiang. The handling capacity is 2.26 times that of 1972. Construction of many more berths is in full swing.

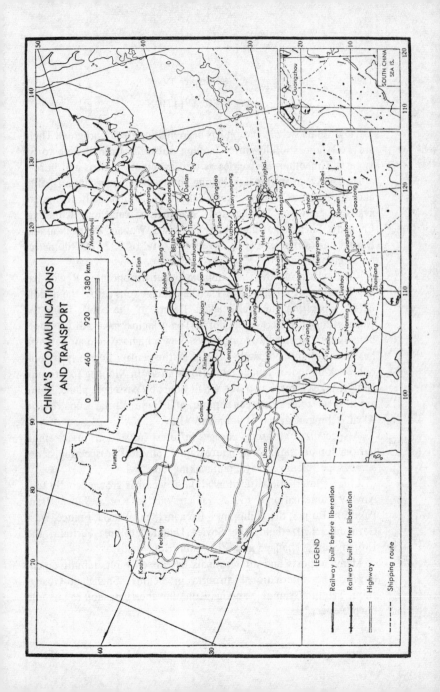

CHINA'S COMMUNICATIONS
AND TRANSPORT

0   460   920   1380 km.

LEGEND

Railway built before liberation

Railway built after liberation

Highway

Shipping route

SOUTH CHINA
SEA IS.

Guangzhou

Urumqi

Kashi
Yecheng
Burang
Lhasa
Golmud
Xining
Lanzhou
Chengdu
Yinchuan
Baotou
Hohhot
Erlian
Taiyuan
Xi'an
Ankang
Chongqing
Guiyang
Kunming
Nanning
Liuzhou
Zhanjiang
Hengyang
Changsha
Nanchang
Wuhan
Hefei
Zhengzhou
Shijiazhuang
BEIJING
Tianjin
Jining
Manzhouli
Harbin
Changchun
Shenyang
Dandong
Dalian
Qingdao
Jinan
Xuzhou
Lianyungang
Nanjing
Shanghai
Hangzhou
Fuzhou
Taibei
Xiamen
Gaoxiong
Guangzhou

(5) CIVIL AVIATION

New China's civil aviation has been making steady progress. There are 163 domestic air routes fanning outwards from Beijing to 86 large and medium-sized cities as well as remote regions and border areas. Direct air routes link Beijing and each province, municipality and autonomous region, except Taiwan. Scheduled daily flights are available between Beijing and Shanghai, Guangzhou, Kunming, Chengdu, Shenyang, Changchun, Changsha, Wuhan, Zhengzhou and Harbin. An airline network covering a total of 232,700 kilometres has been built up.

Civil aviation in the vast Xinjiang Uygur Autonomous Region has developed most rapidly. The Tianshan Range runs across the middle of it, separating the Taklimakan Desert in the south from the Gurbantunggut Desert in the north. The principal means of transport here used to be camels and donkeys. Now a highway and air network has been established, with Urumqi as the centre. Formerly it took one week by motor vehicle from Hotan in south Xinjiang to Urumqi. Now it takes a mere two and a half hours by passenger plane. There are also air routes between Urumqi and Hami, Korla, Kuqa, Kashi, Aksu, Yining, Karamay, Fuyun and Altay.

A specialized air group engages in forest inspection, insect elimination, top-dressing, aerial photography, physical prospecting, aerial surveys, petroleum surveys, rain-making, etc.

China's international civil aviation service has grown rapidly too. Now 21 international routes radiate out to Korea, Japan, Iran, Pakistan, Burma, the Philippines, Romania, Yugoslavia, France, West Germany, Switzerland, the Soviet Union, Ethiopia, Britain, the United States, Thailand and other countries.

Many airports and air terminals have been built, rebuilt or enlarged. The international airports in Beijing, Shanghai, Guangzhou, Tianjin, Urumqi, Nanning, Kunming and Hangzhou can handle big passenger jets.

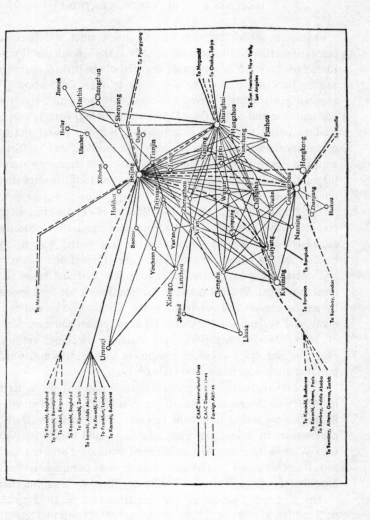

CHINA'S AIR ROUTES

To Pyongyang
To Nagasaki
To Osaka, Tokyo
To San Francisco, New York, Los Angeles
To Manila
To Bombay, London
To Bangkok
To Rangoon

Jiamusi
Harbin
Hailar
Changchun
Ulanhot
Shenyang
Xilinhot
Dalian
Hohhot
Beijing
Tianjin
Datong
Taiyuan
Zhengzhou
Shijiazhuang
Jinan
Qingdao
Xuzhou
Nanjing
Shanghai
Hangzhou
Nanchang
Fuzhou
Wuhan
Changsha
Guilin
Guangzhou
Hongkong
Zhanjiang
Haikou
Nanning
Guiyang
Chongqing
Xian
Yanan
Baotou
Yinchuan
Lanzhou
Xining
Golmud
Chengdu
Kunming
Lhasa
Urumqi

To Moscow

To Karachi, Baghdad
To Karachi, Rawalpindi
To Dubai, Belgrade
To Karachi, Baghdad
To Karachi, Zurich
To Karachi, Addis Ababa
To Karachi, Paris
To Frankfurt, London
To Karachi, Bucharest

To Karachi, Bucharest
To Karachi, Athens, Paris
To Karachi, Addis Ababa
To Bombay, Athens, Geneva, Zurich

CAAC International Lines
CAAC Domestic Lines
Foreign Airlines

(6) POSTS AND TELE-COMMUNICATIONS

A courier service between China's major cities and important points of communication existed as early as the seventh century B.C. Relays of mounted riders carried imperial edicts, official documents and military dispatches day and night to their destination. This imperial postal system served the court, not the public, and it was not until the end of the Qing Dynasty some 2,600 years later that a modern postal service came into being. But the postal and tele-communication service in old China was unsound and inefficient, with few post offices and mainly in the cities and coastal districts. In the rural and frontier areas post and telegraph facilities were almost non-existent.

Conditions changed after Liberation in 1949. An efficient and comprehensive network of post and tele-communication offices was established covering the entire country. The postal system today handles letters, parcels, money orders, newspapers and magazines, and operates telegraph, telephone, telex, and data and image transmission services. Much of the tedious manual work has been replaced by mechanization and automation. The introduction of carrier and microwave systems and the successful development and manufacture of telex, data transmission, long distance telephone automatic exchange and other advanced equipment have transformed China's postal and tele-communication technology.

The construction of a microwave transmission system was started in 1969, with Beijing as its centre. Today it is linked to 26 provinces, municipalities and autonomous regions. It can transmit television programmes in colour and black and white and handle telephone calls. A news-teleprinter service has been established between Beijing and 10 other cities — Chengdu, Guangzhou, Nanning, Kunming, Lanzhou, Nanjing, Wuhan, Chongqing, Changsha and Nanchang.

The distance covered by the postal service in 1983 totalled 4.72 million kilometres. There are almost 50,000 post and tele-communication offices in China today and most rural people's communes are directly linked with post and tele-communication services.

China has direct postal communications with 110 countries and regions, and direct telegraphic communications with 47 countries and regions. Communications with many countries via satellite have started with the building of two ground stations in Beijing and one in Shanghai. The 480-line cable between China and Japan came into use in October 25, 1976.

The making of postage stamps in China has a history of over 100 years. According to 1982 statistics, 420 sets of stamps of various designs — ordinary, special, air-mail and commemorative — have been issued. The commemorative stamps generally mark important political events, such as the inauguration and anniversaries of the founding of the People's Republic. Others commemorate cultural or historical figures, etc.

Special stamps bear designs showing China's economic construction, culture, arts, landscapes, flora and fauna and other aspects of life.

The designing and printing of stamps have been constantly improving. The designs are unique in style, much liked by the public at large and philatelists in particular.

4. MONEY, BANKING AND PUBLIC FINANCE

(1) STATE BUDGET

The state budget is the master plan for public finance. Through it, the state pools and allocates financial resources. It is an essential part of the national economic plan. The implementation of the budget, that is, the day-to-day fiscal operations, is designed to fulfil the needs of a planned economy. All fiscal operations based on the budget are for the purpose of realizing such plan.

The state budget comprises the budgets of both the central and the local governments, the latter including the budgets of the provincial, municipal, autonomous regional, county and autonomous county (banner) governments.

The revenues of the state budget include income from state enterprises, industrial and commercial taxes, salt tax, customs tariff, agricultural tax, and so on. Expenditures comprise outlays on economic development, cultural affairs, education, science, public health, national defence, administration, and so on.

In accordance with the Constitution of the People's Republic of China, the budgets of the central as well as local governments must be scrutinized and approved by the people's congresses at their respective levels.

The state budget is based on the calendar year — the fiscal year starts on January 1 and ends on December 31.

(2) FISCAL REVENUES AND EXPENDITURES

The financial resources of the People's Republic derive mainly from the taxes and profits turned over by the state-owned enterprises and collective enterprises. Among the total amount of fiscal revenues at present, 90 per cent are from state economy and 9 per cent from collective economy. Since the founding of the People's Republic fiscal revenues and expenditures have increased 17 times. Expenditures comprise outlays on development of socialist economy, raising the standard of living of the people in material and cultural life, and national defence. Funds for economic development, education, science and public health are mainly supplied from the public finances. Eighty per cent of the finances are used for developing the economy and raising the cultural and material standards of living of the people. During the past 30 years, socialist construction bloomed with the increase in fiscal expenditure, gaining enormous funds and greatly improving industrial and agricultural

Fiscal Revenues and Expenditures (1952-83)
(in billion yuan)

Year	Sum of Money				Index Number (taking 1952 as 100)	
	Total income	Total expenditure	Balance		Total income	Total expenditure
1952	18.372	17.599	0.773		100	100
1957	31.019	30.421	0.598		168.8	172.9
1965	47.332	46.633	0.699		257.6	265.0
1975	81.561	82.088	−0.527		443.9	466.4
1979	110.327	127.394	−17.067		600.5	723.9
1980	108.52	121.27	−12.75		590.7	689.1
1982	112.397	115.331	−2.934		611.8	655.3
1983	124.899	129.245	−4.346		679.8	734.3

production as well as the level of people's material and cultural life.

(3) TAXATION SYSTEM

Shortly after the People's Republic of China was founded, the system of multiple taxation was carried out. Later it was reformed and simplified and merged serveral times, and at present, there are 14 categories of unified national taxes: industrial and commercial tax, industrial and commercial income tax, state-owned enterprise income tax, agricultural (animal husbandry) tax, customs tariff, salt tax, individual income tax, income tax on Chinese-foreign joint venture enterprises, income tax on foreign enterprises, urban real estate tax, animal slaughter tax, licence tax on vehicles and vessels, fair trade tax and domestic animal trade tax. The latter five taxes are usually called local taxes. Brief introductions are needed for some of the major taxes as follows:

Industrial and Commercial Tax　This tax is levied on all units and individuals which (or who) are engaged in industrial production, communications and transport, purchasing agricultural products, importing goods, and commercial business and service trades, taking the circulating volume of industrial and agricultural products and service trade as the basis for taxation. All foreign businessmen or overseas Chinese businessmen who are engaged in the above-mentioned production or business in China should pay taxes in accordance with this tax law.

Industrial and Commercial Income Tax　Taking the profit volume as the basis for taxation, industrial and commercial income tax should be paid by all non-state-owned enterprises and individuals who are engaged in industrial and commercial business and gain profits from their activities.

State-owned Enterprise Income Tax　For a long time, all the profit earned by the state-owned enterprises had to be turned over to the state. Since June 1, 1983, the system of turning over all profits has been changed into the system of paying income tax. The income tax of the state-owned enterprises shall be computed in accordance with the profits that the units received during the financial year. The tax rates include two categories — proportional tax rate and progressive tax rate.

Customs Tariff It means a tax levied on import and export goods passing through the Customs. Different tax rates are used for different classifications, elements and uses of the import and export goods. In addition, passengers who enter China shall pay duty on their taxable luggage, and receivers shall pay duty on their taxable postal parcels. Tonnage dues shall be paid by vessels which enter China's ports.

Agricultural (animal husbandry) Tax Agricultural tax shall be paid by units and individuals who are engaged in agricultural production and have incomes. The agricultural tax shall be paid at the proportional tax rates according to different areas and chiefly in kind.

Animal husbandry tax shall be paid by units and individuals who are engaged in animal husbandry in the pastoral and semi-pastoral areas. The tax shall be levied in accordance with the number of heads and applies to livestocks including cattle, camels, horses and sheep.

Individual Income Tax The individual income tax rates in 1980 are divided into two categories according to different forms of income: (i) Income from wages and salaries and other fixed income resource under 800 yuan per month shall be free of tax, and the part above 800 yuan per month shall be taxed at progressive rates ranging from 5 per cent to 45 per cent; (ii) Income from remuneration for personal services, royalties, interest, dividends, extra dividends and the lease of property shall be taxed at a proportional rate of 20 per cent.

Income Tax on Chinese-Foreign Joint Ventures The Income Tax Law of the People's Republic of China Concerning Chinese-Foreign Joint Ventures was promulgated in September 1980. It stipulates that the income tax rate on the net profits of joint ventures shall be 30 per cent. In addition, a local income tax on 10 per cent of the assessed national income tax shall be levied. The total income tax rate shall be 33 per cent. There are also many regulations on preferential treatment, such as reduction of or exemption from taxes.

Income Tax Concerning Foreign Enterprises The Income Tax Law of the People's Republic of China Concerning Foreign Enterprises was promulgated in December 1981. Income tax shall be paid by foreign enterprises located in the People's Republic of China on all of their income from production and business operations and on other income. "Foreign enterprises" refers to foreign companies, enterprises and other economic organizations that have establishments within China engaged in independent business operations or in co-operative production or co-operative business operations with Chinese enterprises; and refers to foreign companies, enterprises and other economic organizations that have no establishments in China, but have divident, interest, rental, royalty and other income with a source in China. The income tax on foreign enterprises shall be computed at progressive tax rates, ranging from 20 per cent to 40 per cent, plus a local tax on 10 per cent of taxable income. The total tax rates shall be 20 to 50 per cent. Regulations concerning reduction of or exemption from taxes are also stipulated in the tax law.

(4) THE MONETARY SYSTEM

With the founding of the People's Republic of China, the state immediately took measures to establish a unified and stable monetary and financial system. All bureaucrat-capitalist financial establishments were confiscated and foreign privileges eliminated. Private banking institutions underwent socialist transformation. Currency issuance was placed under the centralized, unified control of the state.

At present, the banking system in China consists of the People's Bank of China, the Bank of China, the Agricultural Bank of China, the People's Construction Bank of China, the Investment Bank of China, the People's Insurance Company of China, the China International Trust and Investment Corporation and the rural credit co-operatives.

The People's Bank of China   This is the central bank of the People's Republic. It not only has sole control over currency issuance, but also acts as the comproller of credit, the centre for the settlement of accounts and the centre for cash transactions. Its essential functions are: to handle the issuance of currency; to readjust the amount of money in circulation; to organize deposits and grant loans; to handle settlement of accounts; and to handle foreign exchange and the safe-keeping of precious metals. The Renminbi (People's Currency, or RMB for short) it issues is the only legal currency circulating throughout the country.

The Bank of China   This bank deals exclusively with foreign exchange, including trade and non-trade accounts and import and export credit. It has branches in places where foreign exchange is handled, and also in Hongkong, London, Singapore, Luxembourg and New York.

The Agricultural Bank of China   This bank specializes in banking business for rural areas throughout the country. Its main tasks are: to handle loans, appropriations and disbursement of funds for farming purposes; to supervise and monitor the use of aid-agriculture funds; and to provide operating guidelines to the rural credit co-operatives and develop rural financial enterprises.

The People's Construction Bank of China   Specializing in the management of funds appropriated by the state for capital construction purposes, this bank is charged with the duties of disbursing appropriations and issuing loans for the state's capital construction. It is also authorized to make short-term loans to engineering units which are short of working capital.

The Investment Bank of China A specialized bank that raises foreign funds for China's construction and handles investment credit. Its main tasks are: to accept loans by international financial organizations; to allocate investment loans in foreign exchange to domestic enterprises; to allocate investment loans for Chinese-foreign joint ventures; and to participate in providing for Chinese investments.

The Rural Credit Cooperatives These are collectively owned financial organizations which, for accounting purposes, act as independent units. Their essential functions are: to handle deposits by individuals and communes, production brigades and teams; to make loans to communes, production brigades and commune members both for agricultural and business purposes.

The People's Insurance Company of China This is a state-owned insurance company. Its main tasks are: to handle insurance for domestic and international property; to handle all kinds of life insurance, including life insurance for groups and simple life insurance as well as insurance for livestock and for crops; to handle all kinds of insurance related to international exchanges; to underwrite all kinds of international reinsurance; and to exchange business with foreign insurance companies. Now the People's Insurance Company of China has established business ties with more than 960 insurance or reinsurance companies in 120 countries and regions.

The China International Trust and Investment Corporation This is a state-owned enterprise that absorbs foreign capital and handles trust and investment. With its head office in Beijing, the corporation consists of the Hongkong Company and the China International Economy Advisory Company. In addition, the China Lease Company and China Orient Lease Company were established in Beijing and are in charge of the rental business both at home and abroad.

(5) BANK CREDIT

In China, credit is the way in which the state raises and distributes monetary funds in a planned manner. The state banks exercise unified control over the credit business for the whole country. They must strictly carry out the credit plans made by the state in granting loans so as to ensure a balance between credit income and expenditures. Without ratification, enterprises usually cannot have relationships of credit with one another.

The credit funds of banks mainly come from deposits of various economic departments and units of the country, bank savings of urban and rural residents, credit funds allocated by the state, annual profits of banks and the issuance of currency. The state stipulates that state-run enterprises, institutions, government units, people's organizations, schools, army units and collective economic units must, in accordance with cash control regulations, deposit in state banks all cash that exceeds the reserve limit and all the income from transferred accounts, and that accounts of transactions beyond the limit must be settled through banks.

Deposits of enterprises occupy an important place in the source of credit funds for banks. The 1981 figure for such deposits was 70.1 billion yuan, about one-third of the total deposits. Furthermore, in recent years, due to the continuous increase of the income of urban and rural residents, their bank savings have grown rapidly. The 1975 figure for individual savings was 15.0 billion yuan; 28.1 billion yuan in 1979; 40.0 billion yuan in 1980; 52.4 billion yuan in 1981, or about 25 per cent of the total deposits; and the 1982 figure was 67.5 billion yuan.

Credit funds are mainly used for the allocation of loans to state-run industrial and commercial enterprises and collective economies. In China, there are two sources of working capital for state-run enterprises. One is financial allocation, the other is bank loans. At present, bank loans to state-run enterprises make up about 30 per cent of the total loans and those to commercial enterprises 60 per cent. It is expected that the working capital for collective economies will be first from their own funds, and only afterwards from bank loans. Loans provided by banks to rural communes and brigades make up 6 per cent of the total loans and those to collective and individual enterprises of industry and commerce in cities and towns about 4 per cent.

Capital construction investments of state-run enterprises had long been provided by financial departments without compensation. In 1979, the state decided that these should be gradually replaced by loans granted by the People's Construction Bank of China. Banks also chose to grant medium- and short-term equipment loans and changed the past practice of only granting loans for working capital. This is an important reform in China's financial and credit system to suit the socialist modernization endeavour.

(6) CURRENCY

The official currency used in China is the Renminbi (RMB), which is issued and controlled by the People's Bank of China.

The denominations of the RMB include: the 1 yuan note, 2 yuan note, 5 yuan note and 10 yuan note, constituting the largest paper notes; 1 *jiao*, 2 *jiao* and 5 *jiao* subsidiary paper notes; and 1 *fen*, 2 *fen* and 5 *fen* subsidiary coins. RMB currency is based on the decimal system. One yuan equals 10 *jiao*, and 1 *jiao* equals 10 *fen*. On April 15, 1980, China also issued metal coins in denominations of 1 *jiao*, 2 *jiao*, 5 *jiao* and 1 yuan.

The state stipulates that RMB can only circulate within the country, and there is a prohibition against carrying it out of China. The circulation of gold, silver and foreign currency within the country is prohibited so that the value of the RMB will not be influenced by fluctuations of the international financial market. The exchange rates of foreign currencies against the Renminbi are determined by the state in accordance with the domestic and foreign market.

5. COMMERCE AND TOURIST INDUSTRY

(1) DOMESTIC COMMERCE

Commercial System At present, domestic commerce is made up of three economic components — state-run commerce with the ownership by the whole people, co-operative commerce with the collective ownership by the labouring people, and individual commerce with private ownership.

State-run commerce is the leading force for the socialist unified market. It plays an important role in the following respects: controlling the resources of all important commodities which relate to the national economy and the people's livelihood; organizing the circulation of commodities throughout the whole country in a planned way; handling the balance between supply and demand; distributing and transferring commodities rationally among various areas; stabilizing market prices; promoting industrial and agricultural production; and meeting the basic daily needs of the people.

The collective commerce, including co-operative shops and co-operative groups as well as small shops collectively-run by residents in cities and towns, engages in retail sales, supplementing the state commerce.

Dealing in all kinds of small commodities, individual commerce is a necessary supplementary to socialist commerce.

On China's market, the above-mentioned three types of commerce co-ordinate, each being in its proper place, in order to promote the circulation of commodities in China. In 1983, state-run commerce made up 72.1 per cent of the total volume of retail sales, collective commerce, 16.6 per cent, and private commerce, 6.5 per cent.

Circulation of Commodities Since the founding of the People's

Retail Sales of Social Consumer Goods

Name	Units	1952	1957	1965	1979	1983
Grain	thousand tons	29,610	37,235	36,820	49,025	75,950
Edible vegetable oil	thousand tons	765	1,030	740	1,045	2,600
Pork	thousand tons	1,704	1,765	2,777	5,980	7,975
Egg	thousand tons	132	259	339	759	1,030
Aquatic product	thousand tons	799	1,424	1,375	1,915	2,254
Sugar	thousand tons	471	879	1,122	3,330	4,439
Wool fabric	thousand metres	3,626	7,094	24,440	105,990	208,044
Silks and satins	thousand metres	30,923	70,908	96,660	353,210	576,263
Knitted underwear	thousand	29,004	202,536	231,996	909,280	1,210,000
Sewing machine	thousand	100	251	897	5,400	10,191
Watch	thousand	385	1,076	1,891	19,444	38,980
Bicycle	thousand	335	847	1,762	9,545	26,207
Radio set	thousand	20	264	836	16,395	30,745
Television set	thousand	—	—	—	1,807	8,340

Republic in 1949, the scale of the circulation of commodities has rapidly enlarged with the development of industry and agriculture and the raising of people's standards of living. From 1952 to 1983, the total volume of goods purchased by state-run commerce increased to 287.6 billion yuan from 17.5 billion yuan, an increase of 17 times. Farm produce and sideline products purchased was 89.06 billion yuan. From 1952 to 1983, total volume of retail sales of social commodities increased to 284.9 billion yuan from 27.7 billion yuan, an increase of 11 times.

Administrative System   Since the founding of new China, the domestic commerce has been led and administered by three main state organizations under the State Council — the Ministry of Commerce, in charge of urban commerce; the All-China Federation of Supply and Marketing Co-operatives, in charge of rural commerce; and the Ministry of Food, in charge of the management of grain and edible oil. During the reform of state structures in 1980, the three organizations were merged into the Ministry of Commerce, exercising unified leadership over the commerce of the whole country. Each province, autonomous region and minicipality under the Central Government establishes a commercial department, and each county a commercial bureau, responsible for commerce in its administrative area.

Under the leadership of the State Council, the Ministry of Commerce is not only the highest commercial administrative organization, but also the agency exercising leadership over the state commercial enterprises of the ownership by the whole people.

To organize and exercise leadership over the national state-commerce, professional companies were set up nationally and locally in the commercial system, such as foodstuff companies, vegetable companies, department store companies, textile companies, hardware and electrical appliances companies, stationery companies and cotton and hemp companies. Independent administrative systems of management were formed from the top level to the grassroots level for each company. The main tasks for these specialized companies are: to supervise and inspect the implementation of the state's principles and policies; rationally distribute commercial goods; help their subordinate enterprises to complete the state plan and improve their management. According to the needs of business operation, all kinds of state-owned commercial enterprises were set up by these professional companies, such as whole sales enterprises, retail sales enterprises and commercial supplementary enterprises (enterprises of storage and transportation, and commercial processing enterprises).

In addition, the General Administrative Bureau of Industry and Commerce and its local branches have been established under the State Council. Their tasks are: to supervise and inspect the implementation of the government's policies and laws; to protect legal business; to crack down on speculation and profiteering activities and other capitalist influences; and to prevent the development of capitalist deviation. Its daily work is to administer the market fairs, register licences and conduct the administration both of trade marks and contracts.

Market Fairs Market fairs have flourished in cities and the countryside for many years. With the development of commodity economy, these fairs gradually became regular ones. After the founding of the People's Republic in 1949, the old fair trade was reformed and strictly administered and since has been reserved as one of the forms of exchange of rural commodities. Since 1978, thanks to the implementation of new rural economic policies, the market fairs, which were forbidden under the influence of the "Left" ideology, have been gradually restored. Some new market fairs of farm and sideline products have been set up in newly-built industrial and mineral areas as well as in cities and towns. Products sold on the market fairs are mainly the peasants' surplus farm and sideline products after they have fulfilled their assigned tasks, or those farm and sideline local products which the state has not planned to purchase, such as meat, poultry, eggs, aquatic products, vegetable and melon, as well as some handicrafts, such as farm tools and other products made by commune- and brigade-run enterprises. People participating in the business operations on these markets include not only commune members and residents in cities and towns, but also some collective economic organizations and licenced pedlers. According to statistics, there were 38,933 rural and urban market fairs, nearly back to the number of 1965. In 1982, market fairs increased to 44,775, among which 3,591 were city fairs of farm and sideline products. The annual volume of business reached 32.8 billion yuan, making up 13 per cent of the total volume of social commercial retail sales.

Market fairs, free markets under the leadership and administration of the state, have played an active role in promoting the development of agriculture and sideline production, stimulating the urban and rural economy, and meeting the needs of the people. However, fair prices are negotiable and greatly influenced by the market supply and demand, so that the planning state market is easily affected. For instance, some peasants, ignoring state policy, sell their products which should have been sold to the state or other products that are prohibited to sell on the market fairs in order to get a good price, making it difficult to fulfil the state plan. Therefore, the state adopted both economic and administrative measures to strengthen its leadership and management over the market fairs. Economic measure means that state and co-operative enterprises participate in the operation of purchase and sale, taking in or sending out goods according to the market in order to adjust supply and demand and stable the price. Furthermore, policies, decrees and administrative regulations are formulated to have a better control over the sellers on the market as well as their goods so as to protect lawful business and ban speculation and profiteering. It is in this way that the urban and rural market fairs will develop healthily.

(2) TOURIST INDUSTRY

Tourist Attractions With its vast territory, the beautiful land of China is well endowed with scenic wonders. The Qinghai-Tibet Plateau, known as the "Roof of the World", the many lofty mountains such as Taishan, Emei, Huangshan and Lushan and the spectacular Three Gorges of the Yangtze River are among these beautiful sights, as are the picturesque Stone Forests of Kunming, the fabled stone caves of Guilin and the lovely West Lake of Hangzhou.

China is famous throughout the world for its rich legacy of splendid cultural and historic sites. There are more than 5,600 important cultural sites under state protection and 24 famous historical and cultural cities.

Having served as the capital of the Yuan (1271-1368), Ming (1368-1644) and Qing (1644-1911) dynasties, Beijing has been left with the Forbidden City, the largest existing palace groups in the world, and the Summer Palace, the imperial garden of the Qing Dynasty. The Ming Tombs, the world-famous Great Wall and the home of Peking Man who lived 500,000 years ago are among the many historic sites.

The ancient city of Xi'an, capital for 10 feudal dynasties, boasts of pottery worriors and horses at the tomb of the First Emperor of Qin (259-210 B.C.), the Greater Wild Goose Pagoda, the Banpo Site where a primitive village once flourished 6,000 years ago as well as the ruins of ancient towns and many other ancient tombs.

In addition, there are the Mogao Grottoes at Dunhuang in Gansu Province, the Yungang Grottoes in Shanxi Province, and the Longmen Grottoes in Henan Province, commonly referred to as three Buddhist art treasure houses. The grand Confucian Mansion, Confucian Temple and Confucian Forest at Qufu in Shandong Province, the hometown of the noted educator and thinker Confucius (551-479 B.C.), are among the many tourist attractions in China, as are the large water conservancy project, the Dujiangyan

Dam, completed over 2,000 years ago, and the world's earliest and largest man-made waterway, the Grand Canal, as well as the 71-metre-high Leshan Buddhist statue, the largest one in the world.

China is a country with many nationalities, and each of the ethnic groups has its unique culture and customs.

Chinese music, operas, dances, arts and crafts and cuisine are famous throughout the world.

The Development of Tourism The tourist industry in China started in 1954 with the setting up of the China International Travel Service, which worked out its plan and established ties with some foreign tourist organizations for the purpose of receiving tourists who travel at their own expense.

The China Travel and Tourism Administration was established in 1964, and has further promoted the development of China's tourist industry. Then, in 1978 tourism entered a new stage, with 1.81 million tourists visiting China. In 1983, over 9.477 million foreigners, overseas Chinese, and compatriots from Hongkong and Macao visited China, including those who came to visit their families and relatives, or were engaged in trade, sports or in exchanges of science, technology or culture. This was 5.2 times the number of those who visited China in 1978. At present, there are 120 tourist attractions and 200 hotels with 70,000 beds serving foreign tourists. In addition, new hotels are under construction.

Tourist Organizations

The Travel and Tourism Leading Group of the State Council Its tasks are: to examine and approve the principles and policies of tourism; to examine the tourist development plan and the construction plan for tourist zones; to be responsible in coordinating the work related to tourism; and to examine and decide on the tourist schedules and check up on their accomplishment.

The Travel and Tourism Administration of the People's Republic of China It is responsible for exercising unified leadership and supervision over the tourist industry throughout the country. Travel and tourist departments are set up in provinces, municipalities and autonomous regions, in charge of exercising the unified administration of tourism in their own areas.

China International Travel Service   Under the leadership of the Travel and Tourism Administration, this service is open to foreign tourists travelling at their own expense. It has branches and sub-branches in provinces, municipalities and autonomous regions as well as cities and prefectures directly under the provinces. The China International Travel Service also has its agencies or representatives in the United States, Japan, Britain, France and other countries, and in Hongkong.

China Travel Service   (Overseas Chinese Travel Service) This office hosts overseas Chinese, compatriots from Hongkong, Macao, Taiwan and foreign citizens of Chinese origin who come to China's mainland for sightseeing, visiting relatives, exchanges of science and technology or for treatment of illness. It has branches or representatives in other countries and in Hongkong and Macao.

China Youth Travel Service   It is the host agency for youths from foreign countries. All kinds of lively activities are arranged to fit the tastes of young people.

6. FOREIGN TRADE

(1) THE BASIC PRINCIPLE OF FOREIGN TRADE

As a component part of the national economy, foreign trade plays an important role in economic exchanges with other countries, serving China's socialist construction. China is a vast country with a population of one billion. Socialist construction must be conducted under the guideline of "self-reliance". That is to say, China must rely principally on her own working people and their wisdom and give

full play to her natural resources and economic foundation. However, self-reliance does not mean autarky or a "closed door" policy.
Acting under the basic principle of foreign trade – independence,
self-reliance, equality, mutual benefit and mutually supplying each
other's needs, China has actively sought to develop trade relations
with the rest of the world. China actively expands her export on the
basis of her growth of production; it imports various goods and
materials, advanced technology and key equipment in order to
promote the development of her economy.

(2) THE DEVELOPMENT OF FOREIGN TRADE

Volume of Foreign Trade Since the founding of the People's
Republic in 1949, China has actively sought to develop trade relations with countries all over the world, and the volume of foreign
trade has increased remarkably.

Total Volume of Foreign Trade*
(in billion yuan)

Year	1950	1952	1957	1978	1979	1982	1983
Total volume of imports and exports	4.16	6.46	10.45	35.51	45.46	75.64	86.01
Imports	2.14	3.75	5.00	18.74	24.29	33.64	43.83
Exports	2.02	2.71	5.45	16.77	21.17	42.00	42.18

*The Customs total volume of imports and exports: 57.0 billion yuan in
1980, 73.5 billion yuan in 1981, 77.2 billion yuan in 1982 and 86.02 billion
yuan in 1983.

In the past 30 years and more, China's foreign trade has basically balanced its imports and exports, a fundamental change from the unfavourable balance of trade which existed in old China. Through planned and organized import and export, it has supported industrial and agricultural production and accumulated some funds for the country's construction.

Make-up of Imports and Exports The make-up of imports and exports has changed considerably since the founding of the People's Republic. Prior to 1949, China's exports included mostly agricultural and sideline products. Since Liberation, industrial and mineral products have taken ever-increasing share, from a mere 9.3 per cent in 1950 to 60.5 per cent in 1982, while agricultural and sideline products have made up only 14.9 per cent of the exports, though the volume of exports of agricultural and sideline products has also increased remarkably.

China exports not only native produce, animal by-products and medicinal materials, but also crude oil, coal, machine tools, hardware, instruments and meters, and other goods, most of which China previously could not produce and had to import. Now many of China's exports have enjoyed prestige on the international market. In addition, China also supplies some countries with complete sets of equipment.

Old China imported chiefly consumer and luxury goods, not means of production which accounted for less than 10 per cent of total imports. After the establishment of new China, means of production have been the main imports, used to accelerate the development of the national economy and to raise China's capacity for self-reliance. From 1952 to 1979, China imported advanced technology and complete sets of equipment for metallurgy, machine-building, automobiles, coal mining, oil exploration, power generation and chemicals, all of which played an important role in forming China's industrial base. In addition, China imported the means of production needed for industry, agriculture, communications and

Make-up of Imports and Exports

Year	Make-up of exports (taking total volume of exports as 100)			Make-up of imports (taking total volume of imports as 100)	
	Industrial and mineral products	Processed agricultural and sideline products	Agricultural and sideline products	Means of production	Means of livelihood
1950	9.3	33.2	57.5	83.4	16.6
1952	17.9	22.8	59.3	89.4	10.6
1957	28.4	31.5	40.1	92.0	8.0
1965	30.9	36.0	33.1	66.5	33.5
1975	39.3	31.1	29.6	85.4	14.6
1978	37.4	35.0	27.6	81.4	18.6
1979	44.0	32.9	23.1	81.3	18.7
1980	51.8	29.5	18.7	78.9	21.1
1982	60.5	24.6	14.9	70.8	29.2

transportation such as machinery, motor vehicles, ships, rolled steel, iron sand, tractors, lead, chemical fertilizer and rubber, and raw materials for textile and light industries.

Foreign Trade Relations Since the founding of the People's Republic, China has established trade relations with 178 countries and regions, of which more than 90 countries have signed trade agreements or protocols with China. In addition, China also signed a trade agreement with the European Economic Community.

In recent years, China has actively developed trade with the Third World countries in Asia, Africa and Latin America. According to statistics of 1982, the volume of imports and exports between China and the Third World countries has increased to US$ 8.653 billion. In accordance with the principles of each other's needs and potential, many countries of the Third World have placed orders with China for tools, machines, building hardware, complete sets of equipment and light industrial and textile goods. China's imports from these countries consisted mainly of agricultural and animal husbandry products, and mineral and chemical products. Presently, China has signed trade agreements with 71 Third World countries.

Among the developed capitalist countries, Japan is China's largest trading partner. Geographical and economic factors have created favourable conditions for the development of trade between China and Japan. The re-establishment of diplomatic relations between the two countries in 1972, the conclusion of the Agreement of Long-term Trade Between China and Japan in February 1978, and the Sino-Japanese Treaty of Peace and Friendship signed in the same year vigorously promoted the development of trade. In 1972, the total volume of trade between China and Japan was only US$ 1 billion, but by 1982 it reached US$ 8.76 billion. China placed orders with Japan for machinery equipment, iron and steel and chemical fertilizer. At the same time, China exports to Japan crude oil, coal, textiles, grain and edible oil.

In 1979, China established formal relations with the European

Economic Community and sent its representative to the EEC. In April 1978, an agreement of long-term trade between China and the EEC was signed. The volume of trade between these two partners rose from US$ 2.1 billion in 1977 to US$ 4.462 billion in 1982. From the EEC, China mainly imports machines, complete sets of equipment, rolled steel and chemicals, while exporting textiles, light industrial products and animal husbandry products, including clothings, sausage casings, hides and pelts, down and fine hair, canned fruits and vegetables.

The trade between China and the United States started anew after the signing of the Shanghai Communique in 1972. In that year, the volume of trade between the two countries was only US$ 13 million, but by 1978 it increased to US$ 1 billion. Then came 1979 — an important year in the development of Sino-American trade relations. In January, China and the United States established diplomatic relations. In July, an Agreement on Trade Relations Between the People's Republic of China and the United States of America was signed. All this ushered in a new period of Sino-American trade relations. The total volume of trade in 1979 reached US$ 2.45 billion. In February 1980, the Agreement on Trade Relations Between the People's Republic of China and the United States of America came into force, and both sides gave each other most-favoured nation treatment. Thus, the 1980 trade volume increased 96 per cent over the previous year. In 1982, the Sino-U.S. trade volume continued to rise to US$ 5.338 billion.

In the 1950s, most of China's foreign trade was with the Soviet Union and some of the Eastern European countries. However, in 1960, the Soviet government unilaterally decided to withdraw all its specialists then working in China and tore up contracts and agreements. As a result trade between the two countries began to decrease. In recent years, the volume of trade between China and the Soviet Union and some of the Eastern European countries (not including Romania) has increased.

Trade between Hongkong-Macao region and China proper is of special significance. Hongkong is China's biggest source of foreign currency and its largest port of re-exportation. Since 1952, a favourable balance of trade between China and Hongkong has been kept. Because of frequent deficits in China's trade with Japan, the EEC and the United States, the Hongkong market becomes all the more important to China's exports. At present, China obtains one-third of her foreign currency earnings through exports by way of Hongkong, and about half of the Chinese commodities from China proper to Hongkong are re-exported to other countries. In 1982, China's trade volume with Hongkong and Macao reached US$ 6.361 billion.

Along with the expansion of trade regions, mutual visiting and friendly activities between the Chinese Government and governments of other countries, and between Chinese and foreign trade circles, have increased. China has participated in many international trade fairs and trade exhibitions outside China, and helped many countries hold industrial, technological and trade exhibitions in China.

Furthermore, the Chinese Export Commodities Fair has been held in Guangzhou every spring and autumn since 1957. By 1983, 54 such fairs were held.

(3) IMPORTANT MEASURES TO EXPAND FOREIGN TRADE

In recent years, China has adopted various major measures to expand foreign trade and strengthen economic co-operation with foreign countries in combination with the country's economic readjustment under the guideline of "taking self-reliance as the principal means and external assistance as a subsidiary".

Use of Flexible Trade Forms to Expand Export Besides maintaining established trade forms, China is concurrently adopting some of the practices common in international trade — using the customer's own brand and trademark on export goods, producing goods according to a sample pattern or model specified by the customer, or with the materials supplied by the customer, and all forms of compensation trade.

China started processing and assembly business and medium- and small-scale compensation trade in 1978. In September 1979, the State Council promulgated the "Regulations Governing the Promotion of Processing and Assembly Business and on Medium- and Small-Scale Compensation Trade Involving Foreign Firms", which provide for exemptions from the Customs tariffs and industrial and commercial taxes as well as other preferential treatment for the above-mentioned forms of trade. The new policy prompted a rapid growth of these forms of trade. By the end of 1983, China had signed more than 1,000 contracts on compensation trade with foreign firms and the total value of imported technology and equipment reached US\$ 960 million.

Establishment of Chinese-foreign Joint Ventures Of the few Chinese-foreign joint ventures established since the founding of the People's Republic, the Sino-Polish Joint Stock Shipping Company has the longest history. The "Law of the People's Republic of China on Chinese-Foreign Joint Ventures" adopted in July 1979 by the Second Session of the Fifth National People's Congress has helped tremendously to develop such Chinese-foreign joint ventures.

The law, which contains 15 articles, defines principles governing the rights and interests of participants in the joint ventures and other major issues. It stipulates that, with a view to expanding international economic co-operation and technical exchange, China permits foreign companies, enterprises and other economic organizations or individuals to join with Chinese companies, enterprises or other economic organizations in establishing joint ventures in China in accordance with the principles of equality and mutual benefit and subject to the approval of the Chinese Government. According to the law, the Chinese Government protects the investments of foreign participants in joint ventures, the profits due to them and their other lawful rights and interests in a joint venture, pursuant to the agreement, contract and articles of association approved by the Chinese Government. The proportion of the investment contributed by a foreign joint venturer shall generally not be less than 25 per cent of the registered capital of a joint venture. The participants in the joint venture shall share the profits, risks and losses in proportion to their respective contributions to the registered capital. Each participant in a joint venture may make its investment in cash, in kind or in industrial property rights. The technology and the equipment that serve as a foreign venturer's investment must be advanced technology and equipment that actually suit China's needs. The investment of a Chinese joint venturer may include the right to the use of a site provided for the joint venture during the period of its operation.

A joint venture shall have a board of directors, with the position of its chairman assumed by the Chinese joint venturer and that of its vice-chairmen by the foreign venturer. In handling major problems, the board reaches decisions through consultation in accordance with the principles of equality and mutual benefit. The offices of president and vice-presidents (or factory manager and deputy managers) shall be assumed by the respective parties to the joint venture. The net profit that a foreign joint venturer receives after fulfilling its obligations under the laws and the contract, the funds it receives at the time of the joint venture's scheduled expiration or early termination, and its other funds may be remitted abroad through the Bank of China in accordance with the foreign exchange control regulations and in the currency specified in the joint venture contract. The wages, salaries and other legitimate income earned by foreign staff and workers of a joint venture, after payment of the individual income tax under China's tax laws, may also be sent abroad through the Bank of China in accordance with the foreign exchange regulations. In addition, the law also has provisions on the production plans of a joint venture, the marketing area of its products, the organizational structure, the employment of staff and workers, managerial authority, the contract period and the procedures for settlement of disputes.

The promulgation of the "Law on Chinese-Foreign Joint Ventures" has aroused great interest among foreign investors. By the end of 1983, 188 Chinese-foreign joint ventures were established in industry, agriculture, energy, construction, tourism and the service trade as well as 1,000 contractual projects under co-operative management, assimilating over US$ 3 billion of foreign capital.

Joint Exploration of Offshore Oil Resources This is a special form of Chinese-foreign economic co-operation. In 1980, China signed agreements on geophysical prospecting in areas in the South China Sea, Yellow Sea and Bohai Sea with more than 40 oil companies of the United States, Britain, France, Italy and Japan. At present, joint exploration and development are under way. China has signed contracts with oil companies of Japan, France and the United States for joint oil exploration in the areas of the Bohai Sea, the Beibu Bay and Yingge Sea in the South China Sea.

Establishment of Special Economic Zones In accordance with a decision by the State Council to adopt special policies and flexible measures for Guangdong and Fujian in their foreign economic relations, certain areas in the two provinces were designated as special economic zones in 1979 to encourage and welcome foreign enterprises, overseas Chinese and compatriots from Hongkong and Macao to invest in all kinds of enterprises. Currently, the special economic zones in China are Shenzhen, Zhuhai and Shantou in Guangdong Province and Xiamen in Fujian Province. All of them are in the beginning stage of establishment.

Absorbing and Utilizing Foreign Loans Now China has signed long-term loan agreements with the governments of Japan and

Belgium. According to these agreements, the Overseas Economic Co-operation Fund of Japan has offered to finance the construction of two ports, three railways and a power station. The Import-Export Bank of Japan has provided loans to be used mainly in the construction of coal mines and oilfields. The Belgian government has extended a loan mainly for the purchase of power station equipment. In addition, China has also signed agreements of loans with Kuwait, Denmark, Italy, the World Bank and the International Fund for Agricultural Development (UN).

In recent years, China has signed various credit agreements with many foreign banks. As China's economy is being readjusted, the amount of imported equipment has been reduced, and most of these credits have not been used.

Absorbing Foreign Funds Through the China International Trust and Investment Corporation Founded in October 1979, the China International Trust and Investment Corporation has made progress in absorbing and utilizing foreign funds, bringing in advanced technology and equipment, and establishing Chinese-foreign joint ventures. It has established the China Orient Leasing Co. Ltd as a joint venture with the Japan Orient Leasing Co. Ltd.

Strengthening Foreign Economic Legislation Apart from "The Law of the People's Republic of China on Chinese-Foreign Joint Ventures", China has formulated and promulgated "The Income Tax Law of the People's Republic of China Concerning Chinese-Foreign Joint Ventures", "The Individual Income Tax Law of the People's Republic of China" and the rules for the implementation of these two laws, "Procedures of the People's Republic of China for the Registration and Administration of Chinese-Foreign Joint Ventures", "Provisions of the People's Republic of China for Labour Management in Chinese-Foreign Joint Ventures" and "Interim Provisions of the State Council of the People's Republic of China for the Control of Resident Representative Offices of Foreign Enterprises", etc.

(4) FOREIGN TRADE ORGANIZATIONS

The Ministry of Foreign Economic Relations and Trade This is one of the components of the State Council of the People's Republic. Under the State Council, the Ministry of Foreign Economic Relations and Trade supervises, co-ordinates and promotes foreign economic activities in provinces, autonomous regions and municipalities as well as in the various departments concerned. Its major tasks are: to develop China's trade with foreign countries; to guide China's economic and technical aid to and co-operation with foreign countries; to utilize foreign funds; to import suitable advanced technical expertise; and to encourage and develop contract projects and labour service co-operation.

Specialized Foreign Trade Import and Export Corporation This corporation includes the China National Cereals, Oils and Foodstuffs Import and Export Corp., China National Native Produce and Animal By-Products Import and Export Corp., China National Textiles Import and Export Corp., China National Light Industrial Products Import and Export Corp., China National Arts and Crafts Import and Export Corp., China National Chemicals Import and Export Corp., China National Metals and Minerals Import and Export Corp., China National Machinery Import and Export Corp., China National Instruments Import and Export Corp., and China National Technical Import and Export Corp.

In addition, there are corporations serving foreign trade, such as the China National Foreign Trade Transportation Corp., China National Chartering Corp., China National Commodities Packaging Corp., China Export Bases Development Corp., and China Trade Consultants and Technical Service Corp.

All these are independent economic entities and independent corporate bodies. They have the power to handle legal affairs related to their business activities.

These corporations have branches in provinces, autonomous

regions and municipalities as well as in major trading ports. Representative offices are also set up in New York, London, Paris, Hamburg, Tokyo and other major foreign cities.

Foreign Trade Corporations Under Ministries and Commissions of the State Council Some of these corporations specialize in foreign trade, the others are concurrently in charge of other business operations. As independent economic units and corporate bodies, these corporations have the power to handle legal affairs related to their business activities. At present, there are 33 foreign trade corporations under the ministries and commissions.

Local Foreign Trade Corporations Presently, foreign trade corporations are established in Guangdong and Fujian provinces and in Shanghai, Tianjin and Beijing. The tasks of these corporations are to unify the management of local import and export businesses and foreign trade transportation, chartering, packaging for export goods, and advertising.

The China Council for the Promotion of International Trade Established in 1952, the council is a non-governmental foreign trade agency. It keeps close ties with China's economic, technical and trade departments, and simultaneously establishes business contacts with many chambers of commerce, economic and trade organizations, companies and enterprises in foreign countries. Guided by China's policies and foreign trade principles, the council undertakes activities in all forms to promote economic and trade relations between China and other countries and develop the understanding and friendship between China and the economic and trade circles of various countries, and between the peoples of China and other countries.

The council has also set up its Foreign Economic and Trade Arbitration Commission, Maritime Arbitration Commission, Trade Mark Agency, and Department of Average Adjustment, which are in charge of arbitrating economic, trade and maritime cases and conducting the registration of trade marks as well as handling the common and single average adjustments. In addition, a Legal Counsel Office has been set up under the council, providing legal consultations for Chinese and foreign clients in cases of economic and trade affairs and of maritime affairs and in cases of arbitration.

Commodities Inspection Agency The Import and Export Commodities Inspection Bureau of the People's Republic of China is the agency responsible for inspecting import and export commodities. The bureau has branches in 29 provinces, municipalities and autonomous regions.

The main tasks of the inspection bureau are: to exercise quality control over all import and export commodities; to unify the management of inspection for all import and export commodities; and to notarize documents related to foreign trade.

At present, legal inspection is conducted in China on all major import and export commodities. Those commodities which have been classified for legal inspection can be permitted for import and export only after they have been gone through inspection and had the certificate signed by the inspection bureau according to the contract and standard regulations.

Chapter V

CULTURE

1. EDUCATION

(1) PROGRESS OF EDUCATION

In pre-Liberation days, education was very backward. In 1949, China had only 207 institutions of higher learning, 5,800 secondary schools (including 1,600 vocational secondary schools and 4,200 ordinary secondary schools) and 289,000 primary schools, with a total of 25 million students and pupils. In addition, the distribution of schools was irrational. Universities were clustered in the large cities — Beijing, Tianjin and Shanghai — and a few of the coastal provinces. Many counties had no secondary schools while even primary schools were rare in border and minority nationality regions.

At the founding of the People's Republic, the government first took over all educational establishments, then made necessary structural changes to some of the universities or departments, increasing the number of science and engineering departments and teacher training colleges to meet the needs of developing educa-tion and economic construction.

The first few years immediately after Liberation saw an upsurge in educational development. Over 54,436,000 students attended either universities or schools in 1952. Compared with 1949, the number of university students increased by 63 per cent, that of secondary school students by 1.5 times, and that of primary school

The Number of Schools of All Levels and The Number of Students and Pupils

	Number of Universities or Schools				Number of Students or Pupils (in million)			
	1949	1976	1979	1983	1949	1976	1979	1983
Institutions of higher learning	205	392	633	805	0.117	0.565	1.02	1.207
Secondary schools*	5,216	194,595	147,266	102,776	1.268	59.055	60.249	46.34
Primary schools	346,800	1,044,300	923,500	862,165	24.391	150.055	146.629	135.78

*Secondary schools include vocational, ordinary and agricultural schools.

pupils by 1.1 times.

Since the late 1950s and early 1960s, the educational department has summed up the experiences of educational work, that "Education must serve proletarian politics and be combined with productive labour", "Enable everyone who receives an education to develop morally, intellectually and physically and become a worker with both socialist consciousness and culture", and formulated regulations applicable to institutions of higher learning and secondary and primary schools with reference to their tasks and objectives, curricula, teaching, scientific research, productive labour and ideological education. Through more than 30 years of development, the total enrollment of students and pupils in schools of all levels amounted to 183.33 million by 1983.

(2) PRE-SCHOOL EDUCATION

Pre-school education has made great progress since the founding of the People's Republic of China. In 1983, there were more than 11 million children in 136,000 kindergartens and nurseries.

Kindergartens and nurseries in new China are run either by the state or by collectives. In the first instance, they are managed by various educational organizations, government organs, institutions · or enterprises; in the second, they are run by neighbourhood committees in cities, or communes, production brigades and teams in rural areas. These kindergartens and nurseries offer either boarding or day facilities or a combination of both. In the countryside, there are also many seasonal kindergartens which open during busy seasons.

The main tasks of these child-care establishments are to help children cultivate desirable habits and bring them up healthily; to guide them gradually to a correct understanding of society and their natural environment; to develop their talents and to teach them to express themselves orally; to do simple arithmetic and encourage their interest in learning as a whole; to inculcate a sense of responsibility, courage, discipline, co-operation, friendliness and good manners; and to teach them basic knowledge and something about music, art and dance.

Kindergartens are divided into three grades: the junior grade admits children from 3 to 4 years of age; the middle grade, 4 to 5 years, and the senior, 5 to 6 years. Children under three are taken care of by nurseries.

A variety of classes such as language, elementary knowledge, arithmetic, music, art and sports are offered and are arranged to suit children of different age groups. Diversified teaching methods are adopted according to the children's ages to help them develop their strong points and overcome their weak points.

Special attention is paid to children's health. The kindergartens have their own medical staff. General physical check-ups are carried out regularly.

Publishing houses for children have been established in Beijing, Shanghai and other cities. Reading materials for children include the monthly magazine *Learning to Speak Through Pictures,* published specially for pre-school children. Many works have been produced especially for children by professional and amateur writers.

(3) PRIMARY EDUCATION

The People's Government has made great effort to popularize education. Primary education is now the rule in most places throughout the country. According to the statistics of 1982, the enrollment rate for school-age children was 93 per cent.

In hilly, mountainous and minority nationality areas where education was virtually non-existent before Liberation, schools of diverse forms have been set up since post-Liberation days. Like the population, these schools are scattered, and in mountain villages with only a few households teachers travel from village to village to teach. To solve the problem of going to school in pastoral areas, the government has set up mobile schools which follow the children of families constantly on the move.

In China, the education system for primary school dictates five years of study, with some schools offering six years.

Children who enter primary school at 6-7 are taught to love labour. Older pupils take part in physical labour for a total of two weeks every year, planting trees, doing simple handicraft work, etc.

(4) SECONDARY EDUCATION

Secondary education in China has made particularly good progress. Junior secondary education is the rule in most big and medium-sized cities.

The system of secondary education will gradually increase from five to six years of study, three years for junior secondary school and three years for senior.

Most secondary school students are non-residents. They receive six days of schooling a week and seven hours each day — six hours for study and one hour for recreation, sports and scientific research, for which the school supplies tutors, equipment and expenses.

The labour department of the government is responsible for the job assignment for graduates of secondary schools in cities. Factories and mines can also admit graduates through examinations.

At the present stage, not all of the graduates of secondary schools are able to go on to universities which can only expand their capacity slowly. In order to train more secondary school students for productive labour, the government attaches great importance to expanding secondary vocational and technical schools. In rural areas, secondary schools specializing in agriculture are being opened to enable more students to take part in agricultural science and technology courses. Schools in coal, metallurgical and oil industrial bases give priority to teaching subjects connected to the industry particular to their areas. Those in smaller cities and towns likewise emphasize the teaching of theory and techniques related to industry, construction, communications, finance, commerce, health care, public services, etc. to prepare students for jobs in their area.

(5) HIGHER EDUCATION

At present, China has 800-odd institutes of higher education in total. By 1983, a total of over 4.11 million people had graduated from China's full-time institutions of higher education. These graduates have made important achievements in academic research and practical work. Famous mathematician Chen Jingrun is a graduate of the 50s.

Before 1949, the departments of institutions of higher education were cumbersome, overlapping and chaotic, and universities and colleges were not properly distributed. After 1952, the government made adjustments in some universities, institutes and departments as well as in certain subjects to rationalize higher education. Engineering universities, teachers colleges and science departments in comprehensive universities were reinforced. Specialized institutes of geology, mining, iron and steel, aeronautics, chemical engineering, railways, shipbuilding, post and tele-communications, water conservancy, motor vehicles and tractors, etc. were started. New disciplines in basic subjects, technological subjects, liberal arts and newly-developed sciences such as nuclear energy, semi-conductors, computer science, automatic control and electronics were added. In recent years, institutions of higher education have strengthened courses in politics, law, finance and economic administration, and also increased the enrollment in these courses.

At present, institutions of higher education, especially those classified as key universities and institutes, are working towards the goal of becoming centres of both teaching and scientific research. Many of the scientific research items approved by the state are participated by institutions of higher education, covering subjects such as mathematics, physics, chemistry, biology, geology and geography, mechanical engineering, pedology, chemical engineering and radiotechnics.

Postgraduate study, designed to train teachers and scientific research workers of a higher standard, varies from 2 to 4 years in length. The principle of postgraduate studies is to combine theory with practice, linking theoretical study with scientific research, using individual tutoring and training by research groups. In 1981, the Chinese Government issued "Regulations Governing Academic Degrees of the People's Republic of China" which distinguishes Bachelor's, Master's and Doctor's degrees, according to different levels of study.

The enrollment of university students is based on moral, intellectual and physical qualities. Examinations are set by the state, while the actual organizing of the examination and correction of the papers are taken care of by educational authorities in each province, autonomous region and municipality directly under the Central Government. Key universities have first pick in selecting students.

University education is free, and students with economic difficulties are provided with grants by the state. Upon completion of their education, students are assigned jobs by the state.

Chinese universities have entered international academic exchanges to ensure a better understanding of higher education and scientific developments abroad and at the same time to introduce to the world what has been achieved in these fields in China.

Exchanges include the interchanges of research papers, books, journals and reference material, of undergraduate and postgraduate students, of visiting professors and scholars either giving lectures or carrying out research work in each other's universities on a short-term basis, attending academic symposiums and carrying out joint investigations, etc.

The universities of Beijing, Qinghua, Nankai, Tianjin, Fudan,

Tongji, Shanghai Jiaotong, Xi'an Jiaotong, Wuhan and Zhong Shan (Sun Yat-sen), and Central China Engineering Institute, etc. have established ties with institutions of higher education in Korea, Romania, Yugoslavia, the United States, Britain, Japan, West Germany, Canada, France, Peru, Egypt and other countries. At present over 10,000 students are studying natural sciences, engineering, agriculture, medicine and languages in foreign countries. Many foreign students also come to study in Chinese universities and institutes.

Since 1978, many foreign scholars and specialists have been invited to lecture in China. Subjects for these lectures include computers, programming, automatic control, systems engineering, lasers, microwaves, laser communications, theoretical physics, quantum mechanics, mechanics of materials, applied mathematics, genetics, and languages.

An increasing number of Chinese professors and specialists have been invited abroad to give lectures or do short-term scientific research in recent years. More and more Chinese professors and experts have attended international academic conferences and read papers.

Academic exchanges have given impetus to improving higher education in China, and the government intends to continue and expand such activities.

2. SCIENCE AND TECHNOLOGY

(1) DEVELOPMENT

Many major scientific and technological inventions and discoveries have originated from China throughout history. But continuous invasions by foreign powers coupled with the corruption of domestic rulers over the last hundred years had their effect on science and

technology in China. Modern science was born in China only after
the anti-imperialist, anti-feudalist May 4th Movement of 1919. In the
decades before Liberation it was due chiefly to the efforts of individual scientists themselves that geological and biological research
made some headway, followed later by research in chemistry,
mathematics, physics, geophysics, and engineering.

After the founding of the People's Republic of China, many
scientific research institutes were established, including the Chinese
Academy of Sciences, the Chinese Academy of Medical Science, the
Chinese Academy of Agricultural Sciences, the Chinese Academy of
Forestry, and other natural science research institutes. Research
bodies run by provinces, autonomous regions and municipalities and
by institutes of higher education have also been set up or expanded,
and a scientific and technological contingent nearly 100 times the
size of that before Liberation has been trained. These provide the
foundation for developing science and technology in China.

The period from 1955 to 1958 witnessed major developments in
science and technology. In early 1955, the government decided to
embark on atomic energy research. The following year a 12-year
plan for scientific development, with stress on such new branches of
science as atomic energy, jet propulsion and computer technology,
was drawn up. The main goals were realized five years ahead of
schedule. By the mid-1960s, in some fields China had approached
the world's most advanced levels.

A national science conference was convened in 1978 to accelerate
the development of science and technology in China. The eight-year
(1978-85) plan drawn up at the conference gives prominence to
agriculture, energy resources, materials, electronic computer technology, laser technology, aerospace technology, high-energy physics,
and genetic engineering — eight major fields having a vital bearing on
science and technology as a whole. In 1980, the experiences of the
past 30 years in the fields of science and technology were summed
up and new policies adopted as follows: first, the development of

the national economy must rely on science and technology; second, science and technology must serve the development of the national economy. Chinese scientists are working hard to fulfil this plan.

Some of China's new achievements in the last 30 years are: successful experiments of atom bombs, hydrogen bombs and guided missiles, the launching and return of man-made satellites, the launching of a carrier rocket and the synthesis of ribonucleic acid.

(2) ORGANIZATIONS FOR SCIENTIFIC RESEARCH

The structure for research in China has five parts: the Chinese Academy of Sciences; the research departments in institutes of higher education; the research bodies of various industrial departments; local institutes of scientific research and mass scientific experimental organizations; and lastly, the national defence research departments.

The State Scientific and Technological Commission Founded to plan, organize and co-ordinate all research efforts, it has under it the China Scientific and Technological Information Institute.

The Chinese Academy of Sciences Founded in November 1949, it is the centre for research in natural sciences. After its establishment all existing research bodies were reorganized into 17 institutes, and new institutes founded to do research on nuclear science, experimental biology, etc.

The Chinese Academy of Sciences is today a research centre with some 36,000 scientists and technicians staffing more than 100 institutes engaged in research in many fields such as mathematics, mechanics, astronomy, physics, chemistry, zoology, botany, geophysics, computer technology, semi-conductors, automation and electronics.

The principal tasks of the Chinese Academy of Sciences are: to conduct basic scientific and theoretical research; to conduct research into and develop new branches of science and technology; and to study major scientific and technological problems of a comprehensive nature arising in the course of China's economic development.

The Chinese Academy of Sciences establishes an Academicians' General Meeting, which is the leading body of the Academy. Academicians are chosen from among outstanding scientists of the country. A presidium is elected on the Academicians' General Meeting and is the policy-making organ when the latter is not in session. The Academy's president and vice-presidents are chosen and elected among members of the presidium and assume leadership in daily administrative matters.

Apart from the Chinese Academy of Sciences, there are also number of academies affiliated to various industrial departments. These deal with specialized researches on agriculture, medical science, geology, architecture, the iron and steel industry, railway engineering, post and tele-communications, the textile industry, etc.

(3) THE CHINESE SCIENCE AND TECHNOLOGY ASSOCIATION

The Chinese Science and Technology Association has as its members scientists' and technicians' organizations, including special academic bodies, research societies and associations.

There are over 100 research organizations under the direct jurisdiction of the Chinese Science and Technology Association, such as the associations of Mathematics, Physics, Agriculture and Mechanical Engineering, and the All-China Medical Association. They are centred in large and medium-sized cities and form a mammoth network for academic exchange. The Chinese Science and Technology Association has the following main functions:

To sponsor and organize scientific and technological exchanges, convene scientific conferences, publish academic journals and papers, and summarize and exchange results and experiences;

To popularize scientific and technological knowledge, sponsor and organize scientific and technological activities for young people, and help carry out scientific experiments among the people in general;

To encourage scientists and technicians to make proposals on the country's scientific and technological work;

To forge friendly links with scientific and technological institutions and individual scientists and technicians abroad, and promote international exchanges in science and technology.

(4) POPULARIZATION OF SCIENCE AND TECHNOLOGY

In addition to training scientists and technicians in regular institutes, much attention is paid to popularizing scientific and technological knowledge to the public and promoting popular scientific and technological activities. The disseminated targets range from children, young students, workers and peasants, to cadres and administrative personnel, and the subject matter ranges from such basics as mathematics, physics, chemistry, biology and geography to astronomy, meteorology, geology, medicine and health, and environmental protection. The public is also being acquainted with advanced technology such as electronic computers, principles and applications of lasers, and comprehensive utilization of natural and energy resources.

Popularization of science and technology in China takes many forms, but essentially it is carried out in the following ways:

1) *Forums.* The China Science and Technology Association and its affiliated societies and planetariums, museums of natural sciences and other such bodies frequently arrange lectures and exhibitions on various fields of science and technology. Radio and TV stations broadcast science and technological programmes.

2) *Production and showing of scientific and educational films.* China has two special studios, one in Beijing and another in Shanghai, producing such films. Some provinces, municipalities, autonomous regions and central industrial departments also produce

scientific and educational films. The Ministry of Agriculture, Animal Husbandry and Fishery has its own studio producing films on agricultural topics. Every year, these units produce between them about 400 scientific and educational films for countrywide distribution.

3) *Science and technological publications.* Many government departments and popular organizations, such as the Popular Science Publishing House under the China Science and Technology Association, and national and local publishers put out books and journals for the public on science and technological subjects. Large-circulation science journals are *Science Pictorial, Scientific Experiment* and *Knowledge Is Strength.* Some societies affiliated to the China Science and Technology Association put out their own journals for the general public, such as *Aeronautical Knowledge* and *Radiotechnics.*

4) *Organizing scientific and technological activities for young people.* These activities are varied and take many forms. There are, for the interested, radio, aeroplane modelling, meteorology, biology and astronomy groups. There are extra-curricular science and technology classes centred on the basic sciences, applied sciences and new technologies. Also held are meetings between scientists and young people, lectures and competitions in mathematics, physics and chemistry.

3. MEDICAL AND PUBLIC HEALTH WORK

(1) MEDICAL INSTITUTIONS AND PERSONNEL

Before the country's Liberation, the best medical facilities and doctors were confined to big cities. One of the first government measures taken after the founding of the People's Republic was to build a more rational network of medical centres. Hospitals and clinics with trained staff were gradually established in all parts of the country. Today, nearly all of the rural communes have their medical and health centres, some of them quite well equipped. Currently, the number of hospital beds is 2.11 million. In addition, there are also many simple hospital beds and patients taken care of at home.

A national medical and health network covering cities and villages is being built, with the aim of providing each county with a general hospital, a health and anti-epidemic station, a child and maternity clinic, and a medicine examination centre; and each commune with a health centre, each production brigade with a medical station or clinic. Bare-foot doctors are trained to staff the growing numbers of medical stations. These are part-time personnel, mostly young peasants with some basic medical training. They are not professional medical workers and generally spend part of their time doing farming. In the southern part of China, they often work barefoot in the paddy-field, so people call them bare-foot doctors.

Figures in 1983 showed that China had 3.25 million full-time doctors and medical workers, 7.4 times the number in 1949, in addition to some 1.34 million locally trained paramedics and 2.19 million health workers and midwives working part time.

(2) SANITATION DRIVES

The government has consistantly organized mass campaigns to improve hygiene and control and eliminate diseases since the founding of the People's Republic. Strong leadership is provided by the health and sanitation campaign committees at the central and local levels. Disease prevention is the watchword, and a tremendous amount of work has been done. All this has helped to improve environmental hygiene and public health in general.

Extensive and intensive efforts have been undertaken by the state to control infectious, parasitic and endemic diseases. Smallpox,

Number of Medical Institutions, Beds and Medical Personnel in China

	1949	1952	1957	1965	1975	1979	1983
Medical Institutions							
Total number	3,670	38,987	122,954	244,266	151,733	176,793	196,017
Number of hospitals	2,600	3,540	4,179	42,711	62,425	65,009	66,662
Medical Personnel (*in thousand*)							
Total number	505	690	1,039	1,532	2,057	2,642	3,253
Number of doctors	363	425	547	763	878	1,088	1,353
Number of hospital beds	80	160	295	766	1,598	1,932	2,110

plague, cholera, venereal diseases and kala-azar have been eliminated or virtually eliminated. The incidence of other diseases including occupational diseases has been lowered, the morbidity and mortality rates for some having fallen sharply. Encouraging results have been obtained in treating schistosomiasis (flukeworm infection), which was considered incurable before Liberation. In 1958, Yujiang in Jiangxi Province was the first snail-infested county in China to virtually eliminate this disease. It was followed by over 200 other counties. Headway has also been made in controlling and treating malaria, filariasis and ankylostomiasis.

(3) MEDICAL AND WELFARE SERVICE

All government functionaries, and urban and mine workers and staff enjoy free medical care when sick or injured. They pay no health insurance premiums. When injured at work, they also get a subsidy for food during the period of hospitalization. Those disabled at work draw a full wage, and this applies also to short-term sick leave and maternity leave.

This regulation has been carried out since 1951, at first only applied to employees of state enterprises, but now free medical care has been extended, with the growth of the national economy, to all state functionaries, cultural, educational and public health establishments as well as members of the armed forces, disabled ex-servicemen and university students. Costs for part of the medical treatment for lineal dependents of employees of state enterprises are also covered by the state.

Huge sums are earmarked by the state every year to set up and run public health and medical establishments. And the price of many medicines has been substantially lowered on several occasions.

Many state-run sanatoria and rest homes have been built in scenic centres. Model workers and workers in hazardous occupations have priority at these places free of charge.

In the countryside, co-operative medical services based on voluntary and mutual aid among the peasants are funded mainly by the commune and production brigade, though each commune member pays a small sum each year into the fund. If a commune member is referred by his medical unit to the commune clinic or county hospital for treatment, his medical expenses are partly or fully covered by the co-operative medical fund. The co-operative medical service is a kind of public welfare for peasants. The production brigades with co-operative medical service makes up 53 per cent of the total production brigades. After carrying out the responsibility system of production, the rural economy has developed very fast, and the type of system and organization of medical service has been changed significantly.

Urban health and medical establishments and those of the People's Liberation Army frequently send out mobile medical teams to rural and remote areas to treat the sick and organize training classes for rural paramedics.

The health of women and children receives special attention. In addition to gynaecological, obstetric and paediatric departments in general hospitals, there are maternity and children's hospitals, maternity and children's clinics and stations. In both urban and rural areas, allowances are made for working women and periodical health checks carried out for the early detection and treatment of the more common diseases.

As a rule, all infants and children in the cities and villages are given BCG and anti-poliomyelitis vaccines and inoculated against smallpox, diphtheria, whooping cough and measles free of charge. In many places periodical physical check-ups are given to children. Complicated surveys were made in 1980 among 249,000 children in 16 provinces, municipalities and autonomous regions. This helped to give a clearer picture of how Chinese children are developing.

(4) ACHIEVEMENTS IN MEDICAL RESEARCH

Chinese medicine and pharmacology go back a long way in time and are an important part of China's splendid cultural heritage.

In addition to drugs, for example, acupuncture and moxibustion, pneumotherapy and deep breathing exercises are used. Chinese medical workers have studied, systematized and improved on many aspects of traditional medicine and pharmacology over the past three decades. They are making exploratory efforts to establish a new system of Chinese medicine and pharmacology which will assimilate what is useful from the Western school of medicine.

The combination of Chinese and Western medicines has proved remarkably successful in lowering the incidence of some common and recurrent diseases and even effecting cures in some serious cases. Acute abdominal cases, such as acute appendicitis, acute pancreatitis, ectopic pregnancy, perforated ulcer, intestinal obstruction, infection of the bile duct, stones in the bile duct and urinary stones, can now be treated without resort to surgery.

A new development in traumatic orthopaedics is the application of traditional Chinese and Western methods of treatment for fractures and joint injuries. This involves immobilizing the injured limb with small, light mobile splints, applying a poultice and prescribing light exercises at an early stage to hasten healing. All this in conjunction with oral traditional Chinese medicine. Since 1958, a hospital in Tianjin has treated cases of fractures of the limb bones using this method and found that healing occurred in about half the time normally required using total fixation with plaster cast. Studies are underway to apply this method to more complicated open bone fractures and fractures near joints.

Another major development in integrating traditional Chinese with Western medicines is the induction of anaesthesia by acupuncture, the insertion of fine metal needles at certain points on the body, which is being employed more and more in clinical practice even as intensive research goes on. It is now used in head, neck, chest and abdominal surgery. Good results have also been obtained in such major operations as cardiac surgery under direct vision with extracorporeal circulation, and in replantation of severed limbs.

Replantation of severed limbs and digits and autotransplantation of limbs are other recent achievements in Chinese medical practice. The first successful reattachment of a completely severed right hand of a worker was performed in 1963 by the Shanghai No. 6 People's Hospital, and similar surgery has been successfully repeated many times. The success stimulated the training of surgical teams in other large cities and led to similar results in other hospitals. In 1977, the Huashan Hospital in Shanghai successfully homotransplanted a complete knee joint with blood vessels and nerves attached to restore the function of a worker's left leg paralysed for nearly four years.

Treatment for extensive burns is another field worth mentioning. The life of a woman with burns covering her whole body (94 per cent were third degree burns) was saved by a hospital in Shanghai. In another operation, the Jishuitan Hospital in Beijing carried out transplantation of blood vessels on a patient with electric deep burns on a forearm and wrist to rebuild circulation and restore the function of the hand. In addition, a series of research projects have been completed in pre-clinical medicine, radio-active medicine and clinical treatment for cardiovascular, parasitic and epidemic diseases, eye, skin and infectious diseases as well as early diagnosis of liver cancer.

(5) FAMILY PLANNING

The government encourages family planning for a controlled increase in population. In heavily populated areas, birth control methods are extensively publicized, and family planning is advocated to bring this about.

Conversely, in sparsely peopled areas inhabited by minority nationalities more children per family are encouraged.

Contraceptive pills, condoms and intra-uterine devices are free and easily obtained. Advice and consultation are available without charge at special birth control clinics, and surgical sterilization is done at state expenses. State employees and enterprise workers who choose to be sterilized receive their normal wages during post operative recuperation. Commune members are given subsidies. Couples with only one child are encouraged not to have more by a system of monetary awards and priorities. Again this does not apply among the minority nationalities, who are encouraged to have more children. At the same time, more welfare services are being introduced to benefit elderly people who are childless.

From 1949 to 1979 the annual population growth rate was around 20 per thousand. In 1983 the national population growth rate was 11.5 per thousand. The goal is to bring the annual population growth rate down to about 5 per thousand by 1985.

4. SPORTS

In the past, the Chinese people were called "the sick men of East Asia". Not one Chinese name can be found among the top world-class athletes or world-record holders in competitive sports before 1949.

The founding of the People's Republic of China, in 1949, brought fundamental changes to the field of sports, and the skills of Chinese athletes improved quickly. By 1983, Chinese athletes had broken or surpassed 264 world records, and they had won 122 world championship titles.

(1) PUBLIC SPORTS

Sports of a mass character can now be found in both cities and countryside. Sports in schools occupy a particularly important position. There are now 200 million young people and children studying in schools and universities, and physical education is an integral part of their educational programme. School sports assure that students develop in an all-round way — morally, intellectually and physically. University, secondary and primary school students are required to attend two periods of physical education classes and to participate in extra-curricular sports activities at least twice each week. In addition, they are expected to take part in morning exercises and exercises during the breaks between classes.

Sports teams have been organized in all schools and universities, and many of them have become exceptionally proficient in particular types of sports. The northeastern city of Dalian, for example, is noted for football, a popular sport in the city's 500-plus secondary and primary schools. About 1,000 football players have been provided by Dalian for national, provincial and city teams.

"National Standards of Physical Fitness" have been implemented in schools and colleges. By the end of 1981, there were more than 90 million people who had met these standards of fitness.

Since 1951, the government has successively promulgated six sets of exercises for adults, four sets for teenagers and six sets for children. Special exercises have been designed for workers. The government stipulates that factories, mines, other enterprises and offices offer two 10 to 20-minute breaks, one in the morning and the other in the afternoon, for physical exercises.

Every summer, mass swimming activities are held on rivers and lakes.

Table tennis, basketball and volleyball are popular in the whole country. Many factories, production brigades, government institutions and enterprises have their own sports teams. Football has achieved particular popularity in northeast, north and south China. Yanbian in Jilin Province and Meixian County in Guangdong Province are famous "homes of football". Taishan County in Guangdong Province, Gaixian County in Liaoning Province and Zhangzhou in

Fujian Province are well-known centres for volleyball.

The sport of running has developed rapidly in recent years. In winter, mass long-distance running is popular, and the participants include not only young and middle-aged people but a number of seventy-year-olds. During New Years and the Spring Festivals many cities organize round-the-city and cross-country races.

In addition, China has developed skill in many traditional sports, such as *taijiquan* (shadow boxing), *liangongshibafa,* (eighteen exercises of martial arts), *qigong* (breathing exercise), and *wushu* (martial arts). The same is true of minority nationality sports, such as horse riding, archery, wrestling, sheep-chasing, yak races, swings and springboards.

Mass participation in sports has not only enhanced people's health, but has also developed large numbers of qualified athletes.

(2) COMPETITIVE SPORTS

At the Ninth Asian Games of 1982, held in India, Chinese athletes won 61 gold medals, 51 silver medals and 41 bronze medals. China ranked first at the Games not only in the number of gold medals won but also in the total number of medals, which shows that China has become strong in Asian sports. But in comparison with the advanced world level, China's sports level still falls far short, especially in track and field, swimming, football and tennis.

The following is a brief account of China's participation in international sports competition of 1978-1983:

Table Tennis Beginning 20-some years ago in 1959, the year in which Rong Guotuan captured the men's singles title at the 25th World Table Tennis Championships, China has continued to maintain its lead in table tennis. At the 36th World Table Tennis Championships of 1981, Chinese players captured all titles in the seven events, something that had never happened before in the 55 years' history of world table tennis championships.

Badminton At the First World Badminton Championship, in 1978, the Chinese team won four out of five titles (men's and women's singles and doubles). At the First World Cup Badminton Championships (team events only) and the Second World Badminton Championships (individual events only), held in 1979, Chinese players captured both the men's and women's team titles, the titles in the men's and women's singles and the title in the men's doubles. At the First World Games for Non-Olympic Sports, held in 1981, the Chinese team took four titles in five individual events — the men's singles and doubles and the women's singles and doubles. In May 1982, the Chinese team participated in the 12th International Badminton Championships for the first time. The Chinese team won over Indonesia, seven times winner of world championship titles, by 5:4, and gained the Thomas Cup.

Volleyball At the World Cup Volleyball Championship and World Volleyball Championship, held in 1977, the Chinese women's team finished fourth and sixth and the men's team fifth and seventh. At the Third World Cup Women's Volleyball Championship, held in 1981, the Chinese team carried off the title after winning all seven matches it played. It was the first world title ever won by Chinese players in the three principal ball games — football, basketball and volleyball. At the Ninth World Women's Volleyball Championship, held in 1982, the Chinese team won the championship title again.

Track and Field In 1957, Zheng Fengrong broke the women's high jump world record by clearing 1.77 metres. After that, Chen Jiaquan, a male athlete, finished 100 metres in 10 seconds, in 1965, which equalled the world record at that time. In 1970, Ni Zhiqin broke the men's high jump world record by clearing 2.29 metres.

In recent years, China's track and field sports have made further progress. At the Ninth Asian Games in 1982, the 19-year-old male high jumper Zhu Jianhua cleared the bar at 2.33 metres — the best performance for that event in that year. At the Fifth National Games in 1983, he broke the men's high jump world record by clearing 2.38 metres. In 1981, Zou Zhenxian's triple jump of 17.32 metres and of 17.34 metres won him the gold medal at the World University Games and the silver medal at the World Cup Athletic Championships.

Swimming Wu Chuanyu won first place in the men's 100-metre backstroke competition at the Fourth World Youth Festival in 1953. Between 1957 and 1960, three Chinese swimmers – Qi Lieyun, Mu Xiangxiong and Mo Guoxiong – bettered the men's 100-metre breaststroke world record five times. Further progress has been made in recent years in international competition. Liang Weifen's performance in the women's 100-metre breaststroke surpassed that of the world record holder, an American swimmer named Caulkins, and won her the championship title at the Hawaii International Swimming Invitational Games of 1980. Li Zhongyi, 19 years old, won the men's 200-metre individual medley gold medal at the Ninth Asian Games by 2 minutes 10.93 seconds.

Diving After defeating the world champion, Irina Kalinina of the Soviet Union, 17-year-old Chen Xiaoxia captured the title in the women's platform diving competition at the Tenth World University Games, held in 1979. The Chinese diving team captured three gold medals and one bronze medal in the four events at the Second World Cup Diving Championships in 1981. In 1983, the Chinese diving team ranked first in the total points of men's and women's team events at the Third World Cup Diving Championships.

Gymnastics Competitive gymnastics in China has reached a world advanced level, and a galaxy of gymnastic stars have been developed. The 15-year-old girl, Ma Yanhong, won the world title for the uneven bars at the 20th World Gymnastics Championships in 1979. Two gold medals were won by Chinese gymnasts – Li Yuejiu on the parallel bars and Huang Yubin on the rings – at the Fifth Gymnastics World Cup in 1980. At the 21st World Gymnastics Championships held in 1981, the Chinese team won second place in the women's team event and third place in the men's team event. Li

Yuejiu and Li Xiaoping won gold medals for the men's floor exercise and pommel horse. At the 22nd World Gymnastics Championships, held in 1983, the Chinese team won, for the first time, the championship in the men's team event.

Sports Acrobatics Chinese acrobats first made their world debut at the Fourth World Championships in Sports Acrobatics in 1980. At the Third Acrobatic World Cup Championships, held in 1981, the Chinese team won four gold medals and seven silver medals. The Chinese team won nine championships, at the Fourth Acrobatic World Cup Championships held in 1983.

Weightlifting In 1956, Chen Jingkai broke the world bantamweight clean and jerk record by 133 kilogrammes, thus putting an end to many years in which no Chinese stood among world record holders. By 1980, 12 weightlifters had broken 12 world records in 6 weight classes on 34 occasions. In 1978 and after, the world 52 kg.-class youth records for snatch and for total points were broken by Wu Shude on six occasions. At the 33rd World Weightlifting Championships in 1979, Wu Shude won the title for the snatch in the 52 kg.-class and the first gold medal for China in world weightlifting championships. At the 13th Asian Weightlifting Championships, held in 1981, he broke the world snatch record of the 56 kg.-class by 126.5 kilogrammes.

(3) SPORTS ORGANIZATIONS

The State Physical Culture and Sports Commission of the People's Republic of China It is a ministerial government agency, which gives unified guidance to physical culture and sports throughout the country. Local commissions are responsible for work in their respective localities.

The All-China Sports Federation This is a nationwide mass sports organization, whose task is to promote sports coordination with the government, publicize and encourage popular sports, organize national competitions, and sponsor and participate in international sports activities. It has branches all over the country. Affiliated with the All-China Sports Federation are associations of individual sports and mass sports organizations. At present there are more than 30 national associations of track and field, swimming, gymnastics, sports acrobatics, basketball, volleyball, football, table tennis, badminton, tennis, handball, baseball and softball, weightlifting, cycling, wrestling, fencing, archery, *weiqi* (go), *xiangqi* (Chinese chess), shooting, mountaineering, model aeroplanes, model ships, winter sports, *wushu* (martial arts), etc.

The Chinese Olympic Committee It is a national sports organization empowered with the responsibility to promote the Olympic Movement and its ideal. As the sole organization representing the Olympic Movement in China, it sends delegations to the Olympic Games and maintains relations with the International Olympic Committee and Olympic Committees in various countries.

The departments of education, the Communist Youth League and trade unions in China have their own sports organizations that take charge of work in sports in their own departments.

Twelve physical culture institutes have been founded in Beijing, Shanghai, Tianjin, Wuhan, Guangzhou, Shenyang, Xi'an, Chengdu, etc. In addition to these institutes, there are physical culture departments in more than 100 teachers colleges where a large number of athletics teachers are trained. There are also 2,500 junior spare-time sports schools in the country. Promising children from primary and secondary schools are enrolled in such sports schools for training after class and on holidays. These schools have succeeded in training many first-rate sportsmen and sportswomen.

A national research institute of sports science was established in Beijing in 1958. This was followed by research institutes in some other parts of the country. The Chinese Society for Sports Science was set up in 1980 in Beijing. It has five branch societies: sports science theory, sports training, sports medicine, sports biomechanics and sports psychology.

More than 4,000 stadiums and gymnasiums have been built throughout the country. Some of these are equipped with the best modern facilities. The Beijing Workers' Stadium, with 80,000 seats, the Capital Gymnasium and the Shanghai Gymnasium, each with 18,000 seats, are among the most well known. In addition, there are many simply-equipped sports grounds.

(4) INTERNATIONAL CONTACTS

In the past 30 years or so, China has exchanged sports visits with over 120 countries and regions in the world, involving nearly 60,000 persons in 4,000 groups. Entrusted by international sports organizations, China has organized many international competitions. For example, the 26th World Table Tennis Championships were held in Beijing in 1961, and the First World Cup Badminton Championships and the Second World Badminton Championships were held in Hangzhou in 1979.

In 1979, the Chinese Olympic Committee restored its legitimate seat on the International Olympic Committee. From then on, Chinese athletes have entered the international arena. China has now become a member country of 47 international and 26 Asian sports organizations. For the first time, a Chinese sports delegation took part in the 13th Winter Olympic Games held in Lake Placid, U.S.A., in February 1980. China also took part in the 14th Winter Olympic Games held in Sarajevo, Yugoslavia, in February 1984.

5. LITERATURE AND THE ARTS

(1) LITERATURE

Classical Literature Literature of the period from the days before the Qin Dynasty (221-207 B.C.) to the Opium War of 1840 during the Qing Dynasty (1644-1911) is referred to as classical Chinese literature. The *Book of Songs* composed during the Western Zhou Dynasty (c. 11th century-770 B.C.) and the Spring and Autumn Period (770-476 B.C.) marked the beginning of China's 3,000 years of literary history. *The Book of Songs* is the earliest and fullest collection of poetry with over 300 poems. In the Warring States Period (475-221 B.C.) the great patriotic poet Qu Yuan (c. 340-278 B.C.) wrote his famous *Li Sao* and other poems, marking the first peak in Chinese literature.

In the Han Dynasty (206 B.C.-A.D. 220) Sima Qian (c. 145-90 B.C.) wrote the *Records of the Historian,* an outstanding historical work, which was studied and used as a model by Tang (618-907) and Song (960-1279) dynasty writers.

Poetry flourished in the Wei and Jin dynasties (220-420). Cao Cao (155-220), Cao Zhi (192-232), Ruan Ji (210-263) and Ji Kang (223-262) were outstanding men of letters of this time, and Tao Yuanming (365 or 372-427) was particularly noted for his idyllic poetry. The Southern and Northern Dynasties (420-589) were known for their folk songs. Love songs predominated in the Southern Dynasties, whereas folk songs expressing the people's militancy were a literary feature of the Northern Dynasties. *The Song of Mulan* is the best-known among the latter type.

The Tang Dynasty was both economically and culturally an age of unprecedented flourishing. Its literature, especially poetry, reached a zenith in Chinese history. *The Complete Collection of Tang Poems,* edited in the early Qing Dynasty, comprises about 50,000 poems by some 2,200 poets, of which the most well-known are Li Bai (701-762), Du Fu (712-770) and Bai Juyi (772-846). Under the initiation of Han Yu (768-824) and Liu Zongyuan (773-819), many great works appeared with reforms in literary form and style and became the prose models for later generation.

Influenced by exotic music, *ci*, a form of poetry consisting of lines of different lengths, appeared in the middle of the Tang Dynasty. This new type of poetry developed fully in the Song Dynasty (960-1279). The main representatives of this school of *ci* writers were Liu Yong, Li Qingzhao (1084-c.1151), Su Shi (1036-1101), and Xin Qiji (1140-1207).

The Song Dynasty also had many famous writers of prose and poetry, Wang Anshi (1021-86) and Su Shi of the Northern Song period and Lu You (1125-1210) of the Southern Song being the most outstanding poets. Su Xun (1009-66), Su Shi, Su Zhe (1039-1112), Ouyang Xiu (1007-72), Wang Anshi and Zeng Gong (1019-83), together with the Tang writers Han Yu and Liu Zongyuan, are called the "eight great essayists of the Tang and Song dynasties".

Short stories in the vernacular, or *huaben* as they were then called, appeared in the Song Dynasty. Written in the language of the people, these story-tellers' scripts reflect mainly the life of the people of the middle and lower strata, exercising considerable influence on later fiction.

Zaju, or poetic drama set to music, was the greatest achievement in the literature of the Yuan Dynasty (1271-1368). It spread from the national capital Dadu (now Beijing) and Hangzhou to other parts of China, and had a far-reaching influence on the later development of play-writing and acting as well as on the rise of various forms of operas. Three hundred and forty-five *zaju* plays have been handed down, 63 of which were written by the well-known playwright Guan Hanqing (?-1279). His *Snow in Midsummer* and Wang Shifu's *The Western Chamber* are masterpieces widely read over the centuries.

The Ming (1368-1644) and Qing (1644-1911) dynasties were great periods of fiction and drama. Famous plays of the Ming Dynasty include *The Tale of the Lute* by Gao Ming (c. 1305-c. 1380) and *The Peony Pavilion* by Tang Xianzu (1550-1617); the best Qing plays are *The Peach-Blossom Fan* by Kong Shangren (1648-1718) and *The Palace of Eternal Youth* by Hong Sheng (1645-1704).

Especially noteworthy are the longer novels which evolved from the story-tellers' scripts of the Song and Yuan dynasties. The appearance of such Ming Dynasty works as *Outlaws of the Marsh* by Shi Nai'an (c. 1296-c. 1370), *Romance of the Three Kingdoms* by Luo Guanzhong (c. 1330-c. 1400), *Journey to the West* by Wu Cheng'en (c. 1500-c. 1582) and *Jin Ping Mei* by Xiao Xiao Sheng (a pen-name) shows that novel-writing had reached maturity. The Qing Dynasty featured such works as *The Scholars*, a satirical novel by Wu Jingzi (1701-54), and Cao Xueqin's (?-1763 or 1764) masterpiece, *A Dream of Red Mansions*. The latter is a great work of realism in classical Chinese literature well known throughout the world. Through its description of the rise and fall of an aristocratic official's family and its portrayal of a multitude of typical characters, the novel makes a most penetrating analysis and critique of China's corrupt feudal society. Pu Songling's (1640-1715) collection of short stories, *Strange Tales from the Carefree Studio*, is also a famous work of the Qing period. It takes its material from stories about ghosts and "fox spirits". Through these tales the author censures the evils of the society in which he lived.

Modern Literature Literature of the period between the Opium War of 1840 and the May 4th Movement of 1919 is referred to as modern Chinese literature. Its works reflect in varying degrees many momentous political incidents and the kaleidoscopic events of social life. They played a progressive role as most of them voiced opposition to invasion by foreign powers and exposed the iniquities of the feudal system of the day.

The best-known progressive poets of this period are Gong Zizhen (1792-1841), Huang Zunxian (1848-1905) and Liu Yazi (1887-1958).

Over 1,000 well-known novels appeared during this period. Most renowned among them are the "four great novels of condemnation" — Li Boyuan's (1867-1907) *Exposure of the Official World*, Wu Jianren's (1866-1910) *Strange Events of the Last Twenty Years*, Liu

E's (1857-1909) *Travels of Mr. Derelict* and Zeng Pu's (1871-1934) *Flower in the Ocean of Sin*.

More and more foreign works were translated into Chinese as contacts with foreign countries increased and the Chinese bourgeoisie felt the need to learn more about the West. The leading translators were Yan Fu (1853-1921) and Lin Shu (1852-1924). Over 1,000 novels were translated into Chinese during this period, promoting Chinese fiction-writing of the time and in subsequent years.

Rise and Development of Revolutionary Literature On May 4, 1919 an anti-imperialist, anti-feudal revolutionary movement swept the country. Its main aims were to overthrow Confucianism and promote science, democracy and writing in the vernacular, and this directly helped the development of the new literary movement. The works of Lu Xun (1881-1936), chief figure in China's cultural revolution, laid the cornerstone of this movement. With incisive realism, his collections of short stories, *Call to Arms* and *Wandering*, lash out against the feudal iniquities of the time. His short story *The True Story of Ah Q* is internationally acknowledged as an immortal work in the history of modern Chinese literature. *The Goddesses* by Guo Moruo (1892-1978) is an outstanding example of modern Chinese poetry.

With the founding of the Chinese Communist Party in 1921, the proletariat began to lead the new literary movement. A fact of great significance is that, in 1923, Qu Qiubai (1899-1935) and Deng Zhongxia (1894-1933), members of the Communist Party, along with others advocated "revolutionary literature", and in 1926 Guo Moruo once again brought up this theme. In order to unite progressive writers and oppose the Kuomintang reactionaries' "encirclement and suppression" policy in the cultural field, the China League of Left-Wing Writers led by the Party was established in March 1930, and the magazines *The Dipper* and *Literature Monthly* were founded. It was during this period that Lu Xun fought against the reactionaries with his trenchant polemic essays, becoming a giant in

China's cultural revolution.

Other important works of this period are Mao Dun's (1896-1981) novel *Midnight*, Ba Jin's (b. 1904) *Trilogy of the Turbulent Currents*, Lao She's (1899-1966) novel *Camel Xiangzi*, Tian Han's (1898-1968) play *The Death of a Famous Actor*, Cao Yu's (b. 1910) play *Thunderstorm*, and poems by Ai Qing (b. 1910) and Zang Kejia (b. 1905).

In May 1942, when the War of Resistance Against Japan (1937-45) was being waged, Mao Zedong published his *Talks at the Yan'an Forum on Literature and Art*, which said that art must serve the people, the workers, peasants and soldiers first, and scientifically expounded the relations between art and the people and between art and life. Inspired by this work, which marked the beginning of a new era in China's proletarian literature and art, writers and artists went among the masses, familiarizing themselves with their lives. As a result, a great number of fine works were produced, such as Zhao Shuli's (1906-70) novels *The Marriage of Young Blacky* and *Rhymes of Li Youcai*, Li Ji's (1922-80) long poem *Wang Gui and Li Xiangxiang*, and the opera *The White-Haired Girl* by He Jingzhi (b. 1924) and Ding Yi (b. 1921).

The novels *The Hurricane* by Zhou Libo (1908-79) and *The Sun Shines over the Sanggan River* by Ding Ling (b. 1907) truthfully portray how the Chinese peasants, inspired and guided by the Communist Party, overthrew feudal rule and won emancipation.

Contemporary Literature   After the founding of the People's Republic of China in October 1949, many outstanding works appeared, such as the novels *Builders of a New Life* by Liu Qing (1916-78), *Great Changes in a Mountain Village* by Zhou Libo, *Sanliwan Village* by Zhao Shuli and *Steeled and Tempered* by Ai Wu (b. 1904). A large number of promising young amateur writers have appeared with new works, such as *Keep the Red Flag Flying* by Liang Bin (b. 1914), *The Song of Youth* by Yang Mo (b. 1914) and *Red Crag* by Luo Guangbin and Yang Yiyan. The poems written by

Ai Qing, Li Ji, Wen Jie (1923-71), Guo Xiaochuan (1919-76), He Jingzhi and other poets are particularly popular among young people. Many narrative poems and legends of minority nationalities also appeared; two well-known writers and poets are Malqinhu (b. 1930), a Mongolian, and Li Qiao (b. 1909) of Yi nationality. Most of these works were rooted in real life, faithfully depicting the features of the age and the people's aspirations in a wide variety of forms and styles. They were of great value in leading people to a deeper understanding of reality, elevating their thinking and satisfying many different aesthetic needs. During the period between mid-60s and mid-70s, literature and the arts stopped for almost 10 years. After 1978, literary and art circles put forward a restoration of the tradition of realism to express the real thinking of the people. Large number of middle-aged and young writers have emerged, such as Wang Meng, Jiang Zilong, Chen Rong, Xu Huaizhong, Zhang Jie, etc. Among them, many are woman writers who become well-known among the people, a trait peculiar to the history of new Chinese literature in the recent half century. Over 400 literary magazines published numerous novels, stories, poems and proses which exposed the negative side of political life during the 10 years that brought suffering and grief to the people. Generally speaking, these works reflect real life in various respects. The writers and poets are open-minded, thinking deeply about social problems and life. They also have a wide range of suject matter at hand, and various techniques and styles. In a word, literature in China is on a sound course of development, and will continue to develop and unceasingly explore new areas of experience.

(2) THE ARTS

Film The cinema was introduced into China in 1896, but it was not until the eve of the First World War that China began to make its first film. In 1931, a number of fairly progressive films were produced by writers and artists in Shanghai and other places who were led or influenced by the Chinese Communist Party. These productions included *Wild Currents, The Great Road, Song of the Fishermen* and *At the Crossroads.* During the period from the War of Resistance Against Japan to the War of Liberation, there appeared, through the efforts of film workers in the Kuomintang-controlled areas, another group of films which exerted a great influence on society, such as *On the Songhua River, The River Flows East in Spring* and *Clouds and Moon Across Eight Thousand Li.*

The Yan'an Film Group set up in September 1938 in the liberated areas produced documentaries of the anti-Japanese war and the War of Liberation, such as *Yan'an and the Eighth Route Army, Dr. Norman Bethune* and *Nanniwan.* In the autumn of 1946, the Northeast Film Studio was established in the Northeast Liberated Area. This was the first people's studio with fairly complete equipment.

After Liberation, the Chinese film industry developed rapidly. Ten feature film studios were set up – the Beijing, the Shanghai, the Changchun, the August First, the Pearl River, the Emei, the Xi'an, the Nanning, the Urumqi and the Huhhot studios – and a number of fine films were made, including *From Victory to Victory, A Dream of Red Mansions, Lin Zexu, The Naval Battle of 1894, The Lin Family's Shop, The New Year Sacrifice, Tear Stains, Happiness for All* and *Legend of Tianyun Mountain.*

Progress was also made in other types of film. Chinese animated films have developed rapidly and won many prizes at international film festivals. Chinese animated films are made in a variety of distinctively Chinese styles, drawing chiefly on traditional Chinese paintings, murals, New Year pictures, folk arts and local operas. Some, for instance, have succeeded in reproducing traditional Chinese ink-wash painting on the screen, and *The Tadpole Looks for His Mother* and *The Cowherd's Flute* enabled the masterpieces of noted artists Qi Baishi and Li Keran to come to life on the screen. This was a pioneering undertaking in film animation and aroused much interest in the film world in China and abroad. Internationally, 18 Chinese animated films have won 26 prizes at film festivals.

Technique in scientific and educational films has also improved rapidly. *Yellow Weasel* and *The Hairy Boy* won awards at international scientific film festivals and *The Stone Flies* (Chrysopa perla) won a prize at an international agricultural contest.

In addition, studios making newsreels and documentaries, scientific, educational and animated films and facilities for the translation and dubbing of foreign films were set up in Beijing, Shanghai and some provinces and autonomous regions.

In order to meet the increasing demand, cinemas were built or expanded in the cities, and mobile film-showing teams were organized in factories, mines and the countryside. There are 110,000 film-showing teams and groups at work today in the country.

Opera With a history of 800 years, opera is the main form of Chinese theatre, integrating singing, dialogue, acting and acrobatics into a unique and fascinating art form. Adapted to the needs of depicting different themes, plots and characters, it is a traditional art form with a strong national flavour and is unique in world theatre.

Chinese opera has a rich repertoire including thematic operas, comedies, tragedies, tragicomedies and poetic folk operas. There are 368 different operatic forms in the country, of which some are revived old operas, some are post-Liberation operas and others come from minority nationality areas. Opera troupes number more than 3,000 as against 1,000 in the early years of Liberation. Professional players and other personnel total 200,000.

Local operas have their own peculiar characteristics. Because they are presented with local languages, songs and music, they are particularly popular. Among the best-known local operatic forms staged nationwide are Beijing Opera, *pingju* (found mainly in north China), *yueju* (mainly in Zhejiang Province and Shanghai) and *yuju* (mainly in Henan Province). With a history of over 150 years, Beijing Opera, which originated in Beijing, is the operatic form commanding the biggest following. It combines acting, dialogue, singing, music, dancing and acrobatics, and its roles can be classified in four categories: *sheng* (male), *dan* (female), *jing* (painted face) and *chou* (clown). There are various styles of singing. In acting and acrobatics, different roles follow different patterns, all rather exaggerated, suggestive and symbolic. The actions of opening a door, going up the stairs, rowing a boat or climbing a hill, for instance, are done purely through the mime-like movements of the actors without the help of props. The outstanding Beijing Opera actor Mei Lanfang (1894-1961) was a great artist who excelled in singing, recitation and dancing and had a fine understanding of music, costumes and make-up. This creative actor formed a school of his own which has been very influential in the contemporary operatic field. His masterpieces include *A Woman Feigning Madness, The Drunken Beauty* and *The King Bids Farewell to His Concubine.* Among other well-known Beijing Opera actors are Cheng Yanqiu, Ma Lianliang, Zhou Xinfang and Zhang Junqiu.

Drama   Chinese drama grew up under the influence of culture from abroad. The Spring Willow Society, established in 1906, and the Evolution Company, established in 1910, were the nation's two earliest drama troupes. The South China Society, another drama troupe set up in 1925, played a great role in promoting the development of Chinese drama. Noted veteran playwrights include Tian Han and Ouyang Yuqian (1889-1962). *Thunderstorm* and *Sunrise* by Cao Yu were staged in the 1930s and had a great effect on society at that time. Plays, such as *Put Down Your Whip* and *Going to the Front,* which were often performed on the streets, stirring and encouraging the people to resist the Japanese invaders and save the country. The historical plays *Qu Yuan* and *Twin Flowers* by Guo Moruo extolled patriotism and self-sacrifice and were well received by the people in the Kuomintang-controlled areas.

Since the founding of the People's Republic, both script writing and dramatic staging have developed rapidly. The most influential post-Liberation plays are *Teahouse* and *Dragon-Beard Ditch* by Lao She and the historical plays *Cai Wenji* by Guo Moruo, *Guan Hanqing* by Tian Han, etc.

Chinese drama is becoming an increasingly popular art form as an effective means to reflect everyday life.

Music   Chinese music has a long history. Even in the Shang and Western Zhou (c. 16th century-8th century B.C.) dynasties music was fairly developed. In the Spring and Autumn and Warring States periods (8th century-3rd century B.C.) there were more than 80 different kinds of musical instruments. Later there appeared many periods during which music and culture flourished. Music for songs, dances, ballads, operas and instrumental pieces all had a clear national flavour. *Eighteen Laments,* a piece of ancient music for stringed instruments, has a plaintive melody. The composition *Ambush on All Sides*, a varied and magnificent melody for the *pipa*, a plucked stringed instrument, is a vivid description of an ancient battle. The instrumental music *Evening by a River in Spring* depicting a fishing boat returning home at sunset, sings of the beauty of the land. These are just a few examples of Chinese classical music.

After the May 4th Movement of 1919, a number of fine revolutionary musicians appeared, such as Nie Er (1912-35) who wrote *The March of the Volunteers* and *Song of Graduation*, and Xian Xinghai (1905-45) who wrote *Go to the Enemy's Rear* and *The Yellow River Cantata*. These works are excellent examples of the proletarian revolutionary music of China.

In 1942, a campaign to develop the *yangge* dance — a popular folk dance in the north — and new opera was launched in Yan'an, where the Chinese Communist Party had its headquarters. As a result, masterpieces such as *Brother and Sister Reclaiming the Wasteland* and *The White-Haired Girl* appeared.

After the establishment of the People's Republic, great progress was made in music composition and music theory. The magnificent music-dance epic *The East Is Red*, in which 3,000 people take part, demonstrates the new development in this particular field. At the same time, achievements were made in the writing of symphonic and instrumental music. Many pieces of such music were composed, including *The Evening Party* by He Luting, *Suite of North Shaanxi* by Ma Ke (1918-76) and *Liang Shanbo and Zhu Yingtai* by He Zhanhao and Chen Gang. A great deal of work has been done simultaneously to collect, rearrange and research into classical and folk music. Guangdong and Chaozhou music, noted for their national features, are typical examples. The *pipa* recital *Ambush on All Sides* by Liu Dehai, a famous traditional Chinese musician, was warmly welcomed by foreign audiences when he performed abroad.

In order to train more musicians, the Chinese Government has set up eight conservatories of music with attached primary and secondary schools in Beijing, Shanghai, Shenyang, Chengdu, Tianjin, Xi'an and Guangzhou, forming a comprehensive system of musical education from the primary to the tertiary level. These conservatories have departments of composition, folk music, vocal music, orchestral music and piano. The Central Conservatory of Music and the Shanghai Conservatory of Music also have departments on conducting, musicology and modern opera. Most of the young musicians who have achieved outstanding results in national and international competitions have been trained by the staff of these schools directly or indirectly.

At present there are more than 100 song and dance troupes, opera companies, symphony orchestras, choirs and national ensembles. The Oriental Song and Dance Troupe, set up in the early 1960s, has a repertoire of 250 items from 30 countries and regions in Asia, Africa and Latin America. It helps to popularize songs and dances from these continents and to promote friendship between the Chinese people and the people of other countries.

Dance Chinese dance also has a long history. On the 5,000-year-old coloured pottery vessels unearthed in Datong County, Qinghai

Province, there are three drawings depicting dance. In the Zhou
Dynasty, there appeared full-length dances relating sacrificial cere-
monies in court. One of the poems *The Nine Songs* by Qu Yuan
describes dances on such occasions, which were popular among the
country folk in the state of Chu during the Warring States Period.
Among Han Dynasty stone reliefs and pottery figurines excavated after 1949, many depict interesting dances such as the *Seven-Dish
Dance* and *The Silk Dance*. Dance in the Tang Dynasty reached an
unprecedented level. *The Melody to the Prince of Qin Breaking
Through the Ranks* is a large dance accompanied by music. In the
Song, Yuan, Ming and Qing dynasties, this art assumed very diverse
forms, and some productions have been handed down to the present
time.

After Liberation, more than 2,000 folk dances were collected and
re-edited. The *yangge* dance of the Han nationality is popular in
north Shaanxi, the northeastern provinces, Shandong and Hebei.
Other types such as the *Dragon Dance, Lion Dance, Red Silk Dance,
Lotus-Flower Dance* and *Flower-Drum Dance* are all fine examples
of traditional folk dances.

China has more than 50 nationalities, most of which have their
own songs and dances. The Mongolian *Bowl Dance,* the Tibetan
Guozhuang Dance, the Uygur *Grape-Picking Dance,* the Miao *Reed-
Pipe Dance,* the Korean *Long-Drum Dance,* the Dai *Peacock Dance*
and others are lasting pieces of art with distinctive features of their
own.

A native dance-drama theatre with a distinctive Chinese style had
been built on this foundation, and influenced by foreign works.
Among the successful achievements of this period were several works
based on traditional and modern themes, such as *The Magic Lotus
Lantern*, a fairy tale, *The Small Dagger Society*, which is about a
peasant uprising in late Qing Dynasty, and *Along the Silk Road*, a
story about the friendship between Chinese and foreign peoples in
the Tang Dynasty.

In addition, ballet also gained development. The Experimental Ballet Company of the Beijing School of Dancing, the first ballet company in China, was formed in 1959, and within a few years, was performing famous European classical ballets like *Swan Lake, The Fountain of Bakhchisaray* and *The Corsair*. The first ballet dancers received their training through actual performance. Retaining the original character of ballet, they drew on traditional Chinese dance and made further innovations, thus creating a new type of ballet which depicts the Chinese people's life in a truly native style. The first outstanding programmes were *The White-Haired Girl* and *The Little Mermaid*.

Acrobatics According to historical records, Chinese acrobatics started as early as the Zhou Dynasty and reached a high level in the Han Dynasty. The pottery acrobats excavated in the Western Han Dynasty tombs show such movements as handstands and "crabs" which performers still do today. These lively movements are done to music.

Acrobatics has tremendous popular appeal as many of their movements are taken from life. Items such as *Pole Climbing* and *Flying Tridents* are based on the movements of picking fruit and the hunt. *Shuttlecock Playing* and *Diabolo Playing* came from folk sport and are thus close to life. Through the efforts of acrobats in the past centuries, many highly complex items were created, including *Pagoda of Bowls, Plate Spinning* and *Handstands on Pyramid Chairs*.

After the founding of the People's Republic, professional acrobatic troupes were set up in various provinces, municipalities and autonomous regions. Many new, graceful items have been created, and performing techniques improved. In recent years, greater attention has been paid to stage setting and musical accompaniment so that acrobatics is now becoming a more complete stage art.

The Fine Arts Chinese fine arts date back several millennia. The coloured pottery figurines of the Neolithic Age of 6,000 or 7,000 years ago, pottery pigs and sheep and bone artifacts carved with birds unearthed in Yuyao of Zhejiang Province, and the drawings on pottery pans excavated in Banpo Village near Xi'an are all magnificent examples of ancient sculpture and painting. The unearthed bronzeware of the Shang and Zhou dynasties with exquisite decoration of painting and sculpture represent the zenith of the fine arts in ancient China. The silk paintings of the late Zhou Dynasty, the pottery figurines and horses and murals excavated from tombs of the Qin and Han dynasties, as well as the pottery warriors and horses unearthed from the tomb of the First Emperor of the Qin Dynasty are all marvellous works of art.

During the Western Jin (265-316) and the Northern and Southern Dynasties (420-589), there was an efflorescence of religious art. The magnificent murals and sculptures in the Dunhuang and Yungang grottoes of Gansu and Shanxi provinces, respectively, are regarded as treasure houses of ancient Chinese art.

Classical Chinese painting flourished during the Sui (581-618) and Tang (618-907) dynasties. *Spring Outing* by the Sui Dynasty artist Zhan Ziqian is a famous landscape in Chinese painting history. In the Tang Dynasty many talented artists appeared, the more famous ones being Yan Liben (?-673), Li Sixun (651-716), Wu Daozi, Wang Wei (701-761) and Han Gan. *Riverside Scene on Qingming Festival* by the Northern Song Dynasty painter Zhang Zeduan is still widely acclaimed today. The Yuan Dynasty saw a great development of the painting of ink and wash. In the Ming and Qing dynasties, Chinese painting further developed and many renowned artists and important paintings appeared.

In the field of sculpture, the Tang Dynasty produced exquisite stone human figures and animals. The Yuan Dynasty stone relief carvings in the grottoes of Hangzhou, Zhejiang Province, and at Juyongguan near Beijing are well known. The stone human figures and animals at the imperial tombs of the Ming and Qing dynasties in Nanjing, Beijing, and Yixian and Zunhua counties of Hebei Province are representatives of these two periods.

Beijing University, one of China's most famous institutions of higher learning.

Beijing University campus.

Students in one of the university's laboratories.

Tibetan primary school at class.

Acupuncture and moxibustion are traditional Chinese medical therapies, which have found widespread application after Liberation. Here, medical research personnel are experimenting on themselves.

Wu Huanxing, Honorary Director of the Institute of Oncology of the Chinese Academy of Medical Sciences and a noted specialist in radiology and oncology.

Chinese athletes at the Eighth Asian Games in late 1978.

A simulation experiment in atmospheric circulational hydromechanics.

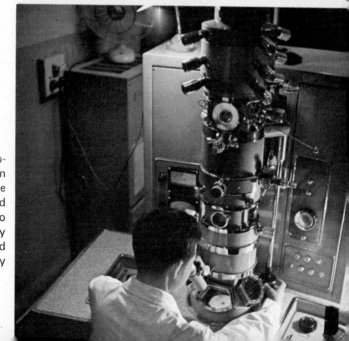

Electron microscopic examination of the superstructure of plastid, to find the causes of albino seedlings of paddy rice, wheat and other plants by anther culture.

A baby panda bred by artificial insemination.

A view of the Yungang Grottoes, Shanxi Province.

Jade suit of a Western Han Dynasty (206 B.C.-A.D. 24) prince unearthed in 1968. Made with 2,498 pieces of jade sewn together with 1,100 grammes of gold thread, this served as his burial suit.

The famous Flying Horse of the Eastern Han Dynasty (25-220) discovered in 1969.

A Tang Dynasty (618-907) figurine.

Scenes from the traditional Beijing Opera,
Women Generals of the Yang Family.

The *Drum Dance* of the Korean nationality.

The *Peacock Dance* of the Dai nationality.

Chinese acrobats.

The six-year-old painter Tan Axi and his paintings. He won a first-class prize at the fourth international children's painting competition held in Finland.

A painting by the late Qi Baishi (1863-1957) done when he was in his nineties.

Horses by Xu Beihong (1895-1953).

Embroidery dates back to very early times in Chinese history. The gold fish (*upper right*) and the kittens (*lower right*) are embroidered on a transparent thin gauze with fine silk thread and can be viewed from both sides.

Chinese art and craft products.

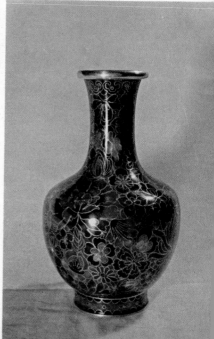

Toys.

Potted landscape is a traditional gardening art in China.

The Nine-Dragon Wall in Beihai Park, Beijing. Built in 1756 with glazed tiles and bricks of seven colours, the wall is 5 metres high, 27 metres long and has 9 coiling dragons on each side.

Wood-block prints first appeared in the Buddhist scriptures of the Sui and Tang dynasties and, along with sculpture, this art made big headway in the Ming and Qing dynasties. Such prints were used in illustrations for books of dramas, legends and novels, as well as in New Year pictures by folk artists and drawings by professionals. Some important books put out during the Ming and Qing periods contain fine water-colour block printings with distinct Chinese characteristics.

Around the period of the May 4th Movement of 1919, posters and cartoons emerged. With the rise of newspapers and periodicals and the adoption of new printing techniques, many pictorials were published.

When the Lu Xun Art Academy was set up in Yan'an in 1938, many revolutionary artists joined it. Artists such as Jiang Feng, Cai Ruohong, Hua Junwu and Gu Yuan created large numbers of works of woodcut and other fine arts.

After Liberation, traditional Chinese paintings, New Year pictures, oil paintings, woodcuts, sculptures, book illustrations and paper-cuts saw further development.

Chinese painting has its own characteristics or advantages. Chinese painters use colour sparsely or abandon it altogether and rely on "line sketches" or "ink and wash" for effect.

At all the art exhibitions held in China, traditional Chinese painting has always occupied an important position. Progress is marked not only in the number of works produced, but more importantly in the breakthrough of limitations of subject matter imposed since the Yuan Dynasty. *Snowstorm in the Wilderness* by Huang Zhou, *Two Lambs* by Zhou Changgu and *Bringing Food on a Snowy Night* by Yang Zhiguang have won international gold medals.

Among the most celebrated painters of contemporary China are Qi Baishi (1863-1957), Xu Beihong (1895-1953), Pan Tianshou (1898-1971), Huang Binhong (1865-1955) and Liu Haisu.

Craft Arts Craft arts have a long tradition in China. As far back as the Neolithic Age, there were jade carvings, Yangshao coloured pottery and Longshan black pottery. In the Shang Dynasty jade carving became a special trade, and this period also produced ivory carvings, glazed pottery and bronzeware. In the Warring States Period, very delicate lacquer and gold-silver ware were produced. Han Dynasty silk and Tang Dynasty tricoloured pottery are well known. In the Song Dynasty, porcelain acquired a high standard, the most famous kilns being in Cizhou (of present-day Hebei Province), Junzhou (of present-day Henan Province) and Longquan (of presentday Zhejiang Province). The blue-and-white porcelain, porcelain with overglaze colours, colour glazed porcelain and cloisonne attained a high level in the Ming and Qing dynasties.

Since the founding of the People's Republic, these arts have developed rapidly. Not only is there now a great variety of works coming out but they are produced in many places. Their wide range of themes reflect China's socialist revolution and construction and the new outlook of its people. There are also works on classical themes including major historical events, stories, legends and folk tales, as well as studies of mountains and rivers, flowers and birds, animals, insects and fish.

Craft arts of present-day China include carving, porcelain, pottery, embroidery, lacquerware, metalware, glassware, craft pictures, woven and plaited articles, coloured lanterns and paper-cuts. Among the well-known products are embroidery, porcelain and pottery. In the field of embroidery, Jiangsu, Hunan, Guangdong and Sichuan are the foremost producers. Chinese porcelain is famous for being white as jade, clear as a mirror, thin as paper and resonant as chime stones. Jingdezhen of Jiangxi Province is called the capital of porcelain, and Yixing of Jiangsu and Shiwan of Guangdong are also well known. Chinese craft arts have often been displayed at international fairs, and special exhibitions have been held in many countries. They are praised by foreign audience, and have made great contributions to promoting cultural exchanges.

6. THE PRESS AND PUBLICATIONS

(1) NEWS REPORTING

Xinhua News Agency The Xinhua (New China) News Agency was established in January 1937, in Yan'an. On September 1, 1944, it started an overseas service in English. At the end of 1948 the first branch outside the country was set up in Prague. In October 1949, after the founding of the People's Republic of China, Xinhua became the nation's official news agency.

Xinhua has a branch in each province, municipality or autonomous region. It has also set up branches in 82 countries and regions, each staffed with a number of correspondents.

Xinhua releases home and world news each day and transmits news abroad mainly in English, but also in French, Spanish, Arabic and Russian.

In Beijing it issues a printed *News Bulletin* every day in Chinese, English, French, Spanish, Arabic and Russian, and *News from Foreign Agencies and Press* in Chinese, English and French.

It has a number of offices in Hongkong and elsewhere, publishing and distributing its daily and weekly journals of broadcast scripts to the world. In addition, over 30 news agencies and newspapers have signed contracts with Xinhua to receive its news directly from teleprinters.

Newsphotos are sent abroad daily by telex and by post.

China News Service The China News Service is an agency serving overseas Chinese, compatriots in Hongkong and Macao and foreign citizens of Chinese origin. It was set up on July 1, 1952 in Beijing to provide news, feature articles and pictures for journals in Hongkong and Macao and journals in Chinese abroad.

The China News Service has branches in Guangdong, Fujian and Shanghai, and one in Hongkong. Correspondents are also stationed in Yunnan and Guangxi.

(2) RADIO AND TELEVISION

Radio   On September 5, 1945, the Yan'an Xinhua Broadcasting Station, the first radio station to be set up by the Chinese Communist Party, went on the air. Later, it changed its name to the Northern Shaanxi Xinhua Broadcasting Station. On March 25, 1949, it moved to Beijing. After the founding of the People's Republic it became known as the Central People's Broadcasting Station (CPBS), transmitting nationwide.

The CPBS broadcasts daily on six separate channels. Two are in *putonghua* (common speech, or standard Chinese); the third, beamed to Taiwan Province, transmits in *putonghua* and the southern Fujian and Kejia dialects; the fourth, beamed to national minority regions, broadcasts in the Mongolian, Tibetan, Uygur, Kazak and Korean languages; and the fifth, for overseas Chinese, is in *putonghua* and the Guangzhou, southern Fujian and Kejia dialects. There is also an FM programme featuring cultural items.

Programmes include news and commentaries, light entertainment, sport, science, hygiene, and regular features for workers, peasants, youth, children and armymen.

There are 122 local radio stations run by provinces, municipalities, autonomous regions and cities under provincial jurisdiction. Practically all counties and towns are wired to broadcasting stations, and these stations reached to most of the rural production brigades. There were 516 relay and transmitting stations throughout the country.

The overseas radio service of the People's Republic of China began transmission in April 1950. Its call sign is Radio Peking (Radio Beijing). Starting with only seven languages, it now broadcasts to the world in 38 foreign languages as well as in *putonghua* and four local dialects.

Its daily broadcasts include news, commentaries and regular and special features for foreign audiences the world over.

Television Beijing Television started broadcasting experimentally on May 1, 1958, and formally on September 2 the same year. It was renamed China Central Television (CCTV) on May 1, 1978. All provinces, municipalities and autonomous regions have their own stations. Most of these transmit CCTV programmes in addition to preparing their own programmes.

The Development of Radio and TV Broadcasting in China

Year	TV stations	Radio stations
1949		49
1957		61
1965	12	87
1975	32	88
1982	47	118
1983	52	122

(3) NEWSPAPERS

The *Renmin Ribao* (*People's Daily*), founded on May 15, 1946, is the main and biggest newspaper in China with a circulation of over four million copies a day. It is printed and circulated simultaneously in all major cities throughout the country. The *Guangming Daily,* started on June 16, 1949, is a newspaper devoted mainly to science and education. Other national papers include the *Workers' Daily,* organ of the All-China Federation of Trade Unions, *Chinese Youth,* organ of the Central Committee of the Communist Youth League, *Chinese Peasant Gazette* and *Chinese Legal Gazette.* Provinces, municipalities and autonomous regions run their own newspapers. Altogether 15.5 billion copies of newspapers at the central, provincial, municipal and autonomous regional levels were sold in 1983.

In addition to all the papers in Chinese, a paper in English, the *China Daily* was started in 1981 mainly for foreigners in China, and is distributed throughout the country and in over 30 countries and regions, with a circulation of more than 70,000 copies.

(4) BOOKS

Since the founding of the People's Republic, publishing work has developed steadily. Integrated national publishing establishments have been set up. Provinces, municipalities and autonomous regions also have their own publishing centres. According to the statistics of 1982, China had a total of 243 publishing houses, of which 121 were national.

Some of the more important ones are the People's Publishing House (works by Marx, Engels, Lenin, Stalin and Mao Zedong, important documents, philosophical and social science works), the Commercial Press (foreign philosophical and social science works, and reference books in Chinese and foreign languages), the Zhonghua Publishing House (classical works), the People's Literature Publishing House (both classical and modern Chinese and foreign literary works), the Foreign Literature Publishing House, the People's Fine Art Publishing House, the People's Music Publishing House, the China Encyclopaedia Publishing House, the Knowledge Publishing House, the Sanlian Book Store, the Science Publishing

House, the Foreign Languages Press, the China Youth Publishing House, the People's Education Publishing House, the Cartographic Publishing House, and the People's Physical Culture Publishing House.

The Foreign Languages Press was set up in 1952 to publish in foreign languages works by Marx, Engels, Lenin, Stalin and Mao Zedong, Party and government documents, literary works, pictorial albums and children's books, as well as informative books on China.

In 1983, a total of 5.8 billion copies of books were printed with 35,700 titles, 23,000 more than in 1950.

Attention has been paid to the publication of philosophical and social science works. In the literary field, a complete collection, selections and separate editions of Lu Xun's works have been published. Literary pieces by established writers such as Guo Moruo, Mao Dun, Ba Jin, Cao Yu and some newcomers have also appeared. Social science works by Guo Moruo, Fan Wenlan, Ai Siqi and others, and natural science treatises by Li Siguang, Hua Luogeng and other reputed scientists have been published. Recently, books for young people are becoming more and more available.

Due attention is being paid to publishing Chinese classical works and treatises on cultural relics. *The Histories of 24 Dynasties,* after 20 years' painstaking work in collating and checking, has now been published in 3,200 volumes containing about 40 million words.

Foreign works in the natural and social sciences and literary works have also been translated and published. Work in this field has been stepped up in recent years.

Since Liberation the number of publications done in various minority nationality languages has grown rapidly. The Nationalities Publishing House was set up in 1953.

(5) PERIODICALS

In over 30 years, the number of periodicals in China has greatly increased. In 1965, there were 790 national, provincial and prefectural periodicals. In 1983, there were 3,415 periodicals, with an aggregate circulation of 1,769 million.

At present, the main national periodicals are the monthlies *Hongqi (Red Flag)*, theoretical organ of the Party Central Committee, *Youth of China,* organ of the Central Committee of the Communist Youth League, and *Women of China,* organ of the All-China Women's Federation. Other major periodicals include *Philosophical Study, Historical Study, Literary Gazette, People's Literature* and *World Literature.*

Seventy-five literary journals were being published in minority nationality languages in 1982.

China publishes six major journals in foreign languages:

Beijing Review is a weekly on political and current affairs, published in English, French, Spanish, German and Japanese.

China Reconstructs is a comprehensive monthly magazine about China, published in English, French, Spanish, German, Arabic and Chinese.

China Pictorial is a large-sized illustrated magazine published monthly in Chinese, Mongolian, Tibetan, Uygur, Kazak, Korean, English, French, German, Spanish, Italian, Swedish, Russian, Japanese, Arabic, Hindi, Urdu, Swahili and Romanian.

Chinese Literature is a quarterly magazine on literature and art, published in English and French.

People's China is a monthly in Japanese, published for Japanese readers.

El Popola Cinio is a monthly in Esperanto, with readership mainly in Europe, North America, Latin America and Japan.

(6) DISTRIBUTION AGENCIES

Xinhua Book Store is the state distribution agency for publications. Its head office is in Beijing, and its distribution network of

5,000 sales departments covers the whole country.

China International Book Trading Corporation (Guoji Shudian) is responsible for distributing books and periodicals abroad. It has connections with over 1,000 booksellers in more than 170 countries and regions.

Waiwen Shudian (Foreign Languages Book Store) distributes books and periodicals in foreign languages. There are foreign languages book stores in Beijing and other big cities.

Books and Periodicals in 1950-83

Year	Books		Periodicals	
	Titles	*Copies printed (in million)*	*Titles*	*Copies printed (in million)*
1950	12,153	274.63	295	35.3
1957	27,571	1,275.44	634	315
1965	20,143	2,171.48	790	440.66
1975	13,716	3,576.24	476	439.28
1979	17,212	4,071.78	1,470	1,183.73
1981	25,601	5,578.3	2,801	1,461.81
1982	31,784	5,879	3,100	1,514
1983	35,700	5,804	3,415	1,769

7. LANGUAGES AND RELIGION

(1) LANGUAGES

The Han nationality, which makes up the overwhelming majority of the population, uses the Han (Chinese) language, which is spoken in all parts of the country. Of the 55 minority nationalities, the Hui and Manchu use the same Han language while the other 53 each has its own spoken language. Of the minority languages, the language of the Han-Tibetan family is used by 29 ethnic groups, including the Zhuang, Bouyei, Dai, Tibetan, Yi, Naxi, Miao, She and Yao, who live mainly in the central-south and southwest; the language of the Altay family is used by 17 ethnic groups, including the Uygur, Ozbek, Kazak, Mongolian, Hezhen and Yugur, who inhabit mainly in the northeast and northwest; the language of the South Asian family is used by three ethnic groups; the language of the Indo-European family by two ethnic groups; and the language of the South Island family by the Gaoshan people. It is not uncommon that several minority nationalities speak the same tongue.

Things are somewhat different with the written languages of the various nationalities in China. Like those of other nationalities the world over, the written languages of China's ethnic groups appeared much later than their spoken languages. Owing to the difference in social development among the nationalities in Chinese history, some of them had had their written languages much earlier than others, some had always shared the written languages of others, and some had never had written languages of their own before the Liberation of 1949, as they were still in a primitive stage of social development. Except the Hui, Manchu and She that used the Chinese script, only 18 of the minority nationalities had their own written languages. Of these, 11 had common scripts, namely, the Mongolian, Tibetan, Yugur, Korean, Kazak, Xibe, Dai, Ozbek, Kirgiz, Tatar and Russian, and 7 had written languages so incomplete that they were not in common use. Some of the nationalities used several written languages at the same time. The Dai, for instance, used four and the Mongolian two. The Manchus had a script of their own, but it is no longer commonly used.

The written languages of the ethnic groups in China vary both in the length of their history and the scope of their use. Among them the Han (Chinese) language has the longest history and the widest circulation. The Chinese characters in use today were evolved from the oracle bone inscriptions of the Shang Dynasty (c. 16th century-11th century B.C.). They are an ideographic script whose pronunciation is not related to its form. Each Chinese character has only one syllable, and there are 5,000-8,000 commonly used characters. As it is not easy to learn and use Chinese characters, reform of the Chinese written language has become one of the major tasks in developing Chinese culture.

The Mongolian language was created in the 13th century, and the Manchu was adapted from the Mongolian alphabet in the mid-15th century. The Tibetan language, on the other hand, was not devised until the mid-7th century. The Uygur, Dai, Korean and Yi scripts also have a long history. The Mongolian, Tibetan, Dai, Korean and Kazak are the most common of the written languages of the minority nationalities.

To carry out a policy of national equality and unity and to develop culture and education among the minority peoples, the government has made extensive work on the spoken and written languages of the minority groups and helped create written languages for the Zhuang, Bouyei, Miao, Yi, Dong, Hani, Lisu, Va, Li and Naxi that had no written languages of their own. It has also helped the Uygur, Kazak, Jingpo, Lahu and Dai peoples reform their scripts.

(2) RELIGION

All three major religions of the world — Buddhism, Islam and Christianity — have followers in China. The indigenous Taoism has a following among some Han people. Freedom of religious belief is a basic policy of the Chinese Communist Party and the Chinese Government, and it is protected by law.

Buddhism Buddhism, also called "the religion of Sakyamuni" in China, was introduced to this country in 67 in the early Eastern Han Dynasty, and began to spread from the fourth century on. By the Sui and Tang dynasties (6th-10th centuries) it was flourishing and, as the numbers of monks grew and spread to other parts of the country, various sects sprang up to combine with indigenous elements.

At the end of the fourth century a monk named Fa Xian (337-422) of the Eastern Jin Dynasty went west from Chang'an (now Xi'an) to seek Buddhist scripture. In his 14 years of travelling he visited some 30 countries, including India and Sri Lanka. He was the first Chinese monk to study in India, and he brought back with him many pieces of Buddhist literature in Sanskrit. He was followed by more Chinese monks, who went to study Buddhism in India, while Indian Buddhist missionaries came to China. The interchange of culture and commodities between China and Central and South Asia steadily increased. The famous Tang Dynasty monk, Xuan Zang (602-664), left Chang'an for India in 627 via Xinjiang and Central Asia and, after 16 years, returned to the same city, where he translated 1,335 volumes of 75 Buddhist sutras into Chinese. He also wrote a book, *Records of the Western Regions of the Great Tang,* which was of great value for the study of the ancient history and geography of India, Nepal, Pakistan, Bangladesh and other parts of Asia.

Another famous monk of the Tang Dynasty, Jian Zhen (688-763), went to Japan at the invitation of Japanese Buddhists. On his sixth try, he finally reached Japan in 754. The next year, in Nara, then Japan's capital, he began to preach and spread Buddhist teachings. He became the founder of the Ritsugaku Sect in Japan.

Accompanying Jian Zhen to Japan were architects, artists and doctors. They took with them a large library and many works of art and did much to stimulate the cultural interflow between the two countries. The magnificent Toshodai Temple in Nara still stands much the same as when it was built under his direction.

Lamaism is an offshoot of Buddhism. It flourishes in regions inhabited by the Tibetan and Mongolian people. Songtsan Gampo, ruler of Tibet in the seventh century, was persuaded by his two wives, Princess Wen Cheng of the Tang Dynasty and Princess Bhrkuti of Nepal, to accept Buddhism. In the late 13th century, Lamaism became a political power as well with the backing of the Yuan Dynasty emperors, and it reached as far as the regions inhabited by the Mongolians.

Lamaism has several different sects, of which the Yellow Sect, founded by Tsong-kha-pa (1357-1419) in the early 15th century, and rapidly grew into the dominant sect with the largest following, thanks to the support of the Qing court.

After the founding of the People's Republic of China, the government began to have the more famous temples restored and refurbished as part of its religious policy. Among these were the Da Ci En Temple in Xi'an where Xuan Zang once translated Buddhist works and the Xing Jiao Temple where his body lies, the Guang Ji Temple in Beijing, the Ling Yin Temple in scenic Hangzhou, the Xuan Zhong Temple in Shanxi Province, the Bai Ma Temple in Henan Province and the Guo Qing Temple in Zhejiang Province. Buildings, sites, objects and relics sacred to Buddhists, such as copies and woodblocks of Buddhist scriptures, images and the famous Dunhuang, Longmen and Yungang grottoes, are all under state protection. A set of important Buddhist sutras whose engraving on 15,000 stone tablets was begun during the mid-fifth century and carried on for over a period of a thousand years, were unearthed from the Yun Ju Temple in Fangshan County, Beijing, after the country's Liberation. Rubbings of the sutras were made and are now kept inside the Guang Ji Temple.

The Chinese Buddhist Association, a national organization of Buddhist followers, was founded in 1953 in Beijing. Its task is to unite with and keep contact with Buddhist followers of the country, collect and collate and make research into the Buddhist doctrine and literature, and to develop the friendship between the Buddhist followers in China and in other countries. The Chinese Buddhist Association has established contacts with Buddhist organizations and individual Buddhists in some 20 countries, and many visits have been exchanged between them.

Branch and local Buddhist associations are found in the larger provinces and cities, on famous Buddhist mountains, in Tibet and Inner Mongolia and the minority nationality areas in Sichuan and Yunnan provinces, etc.

Islam   Islam reached China about the middle of the seventh century during the Tang Dynasty. Arab and Persian merchants of the Islamic faith came overland to northwest China and by sea to Guangzhou and other ports in the south and southeast. These traders spread the teachings of Muhammad and were also the cultural intermediaries between China and their countries. Mosques sprang up in China with the arrival of numbers of Islamic scholars, missionaries and travellers. During the Yuan and Ming dynasties, Islam won more converts in China. The fleet of the famous Ming navigator, Zheng He (1371-1435), had once arrived in the Arabian Pen., and the Moslem members among his crew made a pilgrimage to Mecca.

Today Islam has a large following among 10 of China's minority nationalities, the Hui, Yugur, Kazak, Ozbek, Tajik, Tatar, Kirgiz, Dongxiang, Salar and Bonan. As the government guarantees religious freedom, Chinese Moslems worship and carry on their religious activities without interference, continuing to observe their festivals, customs and habits.

There are famous mosques in Guangdong, Fujian, Zhejiang, Shaanxi, Shanxi, the Xinjiang Uygur Autonomous Region, Beijing and Shanghai. Beijing's Dongsi Mosque was built 500 years ago. In its library are some extremely valuable Islamic books handcopied by imams over the centuries. There are copies of the Koran, philosophical, historical and literary works as well as Islamic classics published in Egypt, India, Turkey and Pakistan. Most of the handcopied works are two to three hundred years old. The rarest work in the library is a handcopied Koran, 680 years old. On the more important religious festivals, the Id al-Fitr and the Corban for example, Moslems including members of the diplomatic corps and other people from Islamic countries working or studying in China come together to worship in the mosque.

In 1953 the Chinese Islamic Association, the national organization of Moslems, was established with headquarters in Beijing and branches where there are substantial numbers of Moslems. It's main task is to make research into the Islamic doctrine, to collect and collate historical data, to develop the patriotism of Moslems, and to promote the friendship and mutual understanding among Moslems in various countries. It organized 11 pilgrimages to Mecca between 1955 and 1979 and visits to a number of Islamic and other countries as well as inviting many Islamic scholars, muftis and notables to China.

Christianity During the Tang and Yuan dynasties, members of several Christian denominations made their way to China, but not in any numbers. In 635 the first Nestorian Christians reached this country from Persia, but Nestorianism was active in China only for about 300 years. It was not until the 13th century that more Christian missionaries arrived, this time from the Vatican in Rome. They too did not succeed in establishing much of a presence.

The Roman Catholic Church sent more missionaries towards the end of the Ming Dynasty. This second attempt is generally considered as starting with the arrival of the Italian Jesuit missionary Matteo Ricci in 1582. After the conclusion of the Sino-Russian Treaty of Kiakhta in 1727, some Russian Orthodox Church missionaries were sent to north China by the Tsar of Russia. Protestant missionaries began to appear in China around the time of the Opium War of 1840-42.

Soon after the founding of the People's Republic of China, Christians and Catholics in China set up anti-imperialist patriotic national organizations. In 1954, the Three-Self Patriotic Movement Committee of the Protestant Churches of China was formed with headquarters in Shanghai. It practises self-administration, self-support and self-propagation in evangelic work. In 1957, representatives of Chinese Catholics formed the Chinese Patriotic Catholic Association, with headquarters in Beijing.

The purposes of the Three-Self Patriotic Movement Committee of the Protestant Churches of China and the Chinese Patriotic Catholic Association are to unite with the Christians and Catholics in the whole country, to actively participate in socialist construction, develop patriotism, oppose imperialist aggression and safeguard world peace. In international exchanges, they adhere to the principle of independence, equality and friendship, and actively promote the friendly visits among the Christians and Catholics and among the peoples of various countries.

Taoism Taoism sprang from the Han nationality and is a uniquely indigenous religion to China. It was founded by Zhang Daoling (?-156). Taoists worship supernatural beings and believe that their particular regimen (including meditation and ascetic practices) can help them attain immortality and get rid of worldly sufferings once for all.

In the early period, Taoism drew its followers mainly from among the peasants. It once rallied them to fight feudal oppression. An instance is the peasant uprising towards the end of the Eastern Han Dynasty, led by Zhang Jiao in what is now Hebei Province. This popular religious leader organized the peasants and led them to revolt under a Taoist banner. Hundreds of thousands joined him and, in 184, the Yellow Turban peasant uprising broke out to shake the feudal empire.

Taoism was embraced by members of the feudal ruling class after the Jin Dynasty. It assimilated elements of Confucian and Buddhist ideas and developed into a great religious force rivalling Buddhism in feudal China. As a religion, it steadily declined after the Ming and Qing dynasties.

In 1957 the Chinese Taoist Association was established in Beijing with the aim of bringing together all Taoists and Taoist scholars of China to study the history and the doctrines of this religion.

Local branches of the Chinese Taoist Association have been set up in the places where there are famous Taoist temples.

APPENDICES

1. COUNTRIES HAVING DIPLOMATIC RELATIONS WITH CHINA

Asia

Country	*Date of Establishment of Diplomatic Relations*
Democratic People's Republic of Korea	October 6, 1949
People's Republic of Mongolia	October 16, 1949
Socialist Republic of Viet Nam	January 18, 1950
Republic of India	April 1, 1950
Socialist Republic of the Union of Burma	June 8, 1950
Islamic Republic of Pakistan	May 21, 1951
Democratic Republic of Afghanistan	January 20, 1955
Kingdom of Nepal	August 1, 1955
Syrian Arab Republic	August 1, 1956
Yemen Arab Republic	September 24, 1956
Democratic Socialist Republic of Sri Lanka	February 7, 1957

Democratic Kampuchea	July 19, 1958
Republic of Iraq	August 20, 1958
People's Democratic Republic of Laos	April 25, 1961
People's Democratic Republic of Yemen	January 31, 1968
State of Kuwait	March 22, 1971
Republic of Turkey	August 4, 1971
Islamic Republic of Iran	August 16, 1971
Republic of Lebanon	November 9, 1971
Republic of Cyprus	December 14, 1971
Japan	September 29, 1972
Republic of Maldives	October 14, 1972
Federation of Malaysia	May 31, 1974
Republic of the Philippines	June 9, 1975
Kingdom of Thailand	July 1, 1975
People's Republic of Bangladesh	October 4, 1975
Hashemite Kingdom of Jordan	April 7, 1977
Sultanate of Oman	May 25, 1978

Africa

Arab Republic of Egypt	May 30, 1956
Kingdom of Morocco	November 1, 1958
Democratic People's Republic of Algeria	December 20, 1958
Democratic Republic of the Sudan	February 4, 1959

Republic of Guinea	October 4, 1959
Republic of Ghana	July 5, 1960
Republic of Mali	October 25, 1960
Somali Democratic Republic	December 14, 1960
Republic of Zaire	February 20, 1961
Republic of Uganda	October 18, 1962
Republic of Kenya	December 14, 1963
Republic of Burundi	December 21, 1963
Republic of Tunisia	January 10, 1964
People's Republic of the Congo	February 22, 1964
United Republic of Tanzania	April 26, 1964
Central African Republic	September 29, 1964
Republic of Zambia	October 29, 1964
People's Republic of Benin	November 12, 1964
Islamic Republic of Mauritania	July 19, 1965
Republic of Equatorial Guinea	October 15, 1970
Socialist Ethiopia	November 24, 1970
Federal Republic of Nigeria	February 10, 1971
Republic of Cameroon	March 26, 1971
Republic of Sierra Leone	July 29, 1971
Republic of Rwanda	November 12, 1971
Republic of Senegal	December 7, 1971
Mauritius	April 15, 1972
Republic of Togo	September 19, 1972
Democratic Republic of Madagascar	November 6, 1972

Republic of Chad	November 28, 1972
Republic of the Upper Volta	September 15, 1973
Republic of Guinea-Bissau	March 15, 1974
Republic of Gabon	April 20, 1974
Republic of Niger	July 20, 1974
Republic of the Gambia	December 14, 1974
Republic of Botswana	January 6, 1975
People's Republic of Mozambique	June 25, 1975
Democratic Republic of Sao Tome and Principe	July 12, 1975
Islamic Federal Republic of Comoros	November 13, 1975
Republic of Cape Verde	April 25, 1976
Republic of Seychelles	June 30, 1976
Republic of Liberia	February 17, 1977
Socialist People's Libyan Arab Jamahiriya	August 9, 1978
Republic of Djibouti	January 8, 1979
Republic of Zimbabwe	April 18, 1980
People's Republic of Angola	January 12, 1983
Republic of Ivory Coast	March 2, 1983
Kingdom of Lesotho	April 30, 1983

Europe

Union of Soviet Socialist Republics	October 3, 1949
People's Republic of Bulgaria	October 4, 1949

Socialist Republic of Romania	October 5, 1949
People's Republic of Hungary	October 6, 1949
Czechoslovak Socialist Republic	October 6, 1949
People's Republic of Poland	October 7, 1949
German Democratic Republic	October 27, 1949
People's Socialist Republic of Albania	November 23, 1949
Kingdom of Sweden	May 9, 1950
Kingdom of Denmark	May 11, 1950
Swiss Confederation	September 14, 1950
Republic of Finland	October 28, 1950
Kingdom of Norway	October 5, 1954
Socialist Federal Republic of Yugoslavia	January 2, 1955
Republic of France	January 27, 1964
Republic of Italy	November 6, 1970
Republic of San Marino	
(Official relations at consular level)	May 6, 1971
Republic of Austria	May 28, 1971
Kingdom of Belgium	October 25, 1971
Republic of Iceland	December 8, 1971
Republic of Malta	January 31, 1972
United Kingdom of Great Britain and	
Northern Ireland	March 13, 1972
Kingdom of the Netherlands	May 18, 1972
Hellenic Republic	June 5, 1972
Federal Republic of Germany	October 11, 1972

Grand Duchy of Luxembourg	November 16, 1972
Spanish State	March 9, 1973
Republic of Portugal	February 8, 1979
Republic of Ireland	June 22, 1979

America

Republic of Cuba	September 28, 1960
Canada	October 13, 1970
Republic of Chile	December 15, 1970
Republic of Peru	November 2, 1971
United States of Mexico	February 14, 1972
Republic of Argentina	February 19, 1972
Co-operative Republic of Guyana	June 27, 1972
Jamaica	November 21, 1972
Republic of Trinidad and Tobago	June 20, 1974
Republic of Venezuela	June 28, 1974
Federative Republic of Brazil	August 15, 1974
Republic of Surinam	May 28, 1976
Barbados	May 30, 1977
United States of America	January 1, 1979
Republic of Ecuador	January 2, 1980
Republic of Colombia	February 7, 1980
Antigua and Barbuda	January 1, 1983

Oceania and the Pacific Islands

Commonwealth of Australia	December 21, 1972
New Zealand	December 22, 1972
Fiji	November 5, 1975
Western Samoa	November 6, 1975
Papua New Guinea	October 12, 1976
Republic of Kiribati	June 25, 1980
Republic of Vanuatu	March 26, 1982

(1) On March 22, 1965 a joint statement was signed by the Chinese People's Institute of Foreign Affairs and the Palestine Liberation Organization. It was agreed that a mission of the Palestine Liberation Organization be set up in Beijing.

(2) The list covers the period up to and including April 30, 1983.

2. CONVERSION TABLE

Length

1 kilometre (1,000 m.) = 2 li = 0.621 mile = 0.540 nautical mile
1 metre (m.) = 3 *chi* = 3.281 feet
1 li = 0.5 kilometre = 0.311 mile = 0.270 nautical mile
1 *chi* = 0.333 metre = 1.094 feet
1 mile = 1.609 kilometres = 3.219 li = 0.868 nautical mile
1 foot = 0.305 metre = 0.914 *chi*
1 nautical mile = 1.852 kilometres = 3.704 li = 1.150 miles

Area

1 hectare = 15 mu = 2.47 acres
1 mu = 6.667 ares = 0.164 acre
1 acre = 0.405 hectare = 6.070 mu

Weight

1 kilogramme = 2 *jin* = 2.205 pounds
1 *jin* = 0.5 kilogramme = 1.102 pounds
1 pound = 0.454 kilogramme = 0.907 *jin*

Capacity

1 litre (metric system) = 1 *sheng* = 0.220 gallon
1 gallon (English system) = 4.546 litres = 4.546 *sheng*

3. DISTANCES BY RAIL BETWEEN CHINA'S MAIN CITIES
(in km.)

	Beijing	Shanghai	Tianjin	Guangzhou	Nanning	Changsha	Wuhan	Nanjing	Hangzhou	Jinan	Qingdao	Xi'an	Kunming	Chengdu	Chongqing	Zhengzhou	Dalian	Shenyang	Changchun
Shanghai	1462																		
Tianjin	137	1325																	
Guangzhou	2313	1811	2450																
Nanning	2565	2063	2702	1334															
Changsha	1587	1187	1724	726	978														
Wuhan	1229	1534	1366	1084	1336	358													
Nanjing	1157	305	1020	2116	2368	1492	1229												
Hangzhou	1651	189	1514	1622	1874	998	1356	494											
Jinan	494	968	357	2284	2536	1558	1200	663	1157										
Qingdao	887	1361	750	2677	2929	1951	1593	1056	1550	393									
Xi'an	1165	1511	1302	2129	2381	1403	1045	1206	1700	1177	1570								
Kunming	3179	2677	3316	2216	1501	1592	1950	2982	2488	3119	2513	1942							
Chengdu	2048	2353	2185	2544	1829	1920	1887	2048	2542	2019	2412	842	1100						
Chongqing	2552	2501	2689	2040	1325	1416	1774	2552	2312	2523	2916	1346	1102	504					
Zhengzhou	695	1000	832	1618	1870	892	534	695	1189	666	1059	511	2453	1353	1857				
Dalian	1238	2426	1101	3551	3803	2825	2467	2121	2615	1458	1851	2403	4417	3286	3790	1933			
Shenyang	841	2029	704	3154	3406	2428	2070	1724	2218	1061	1454	2006	4020	2889	3393	1536	397		
Changchun	1146	2334	1009	3459	3711	2733	2375	2029	2523	1366	1759	2311	4325	3194	3698	1841	702	305	
Harbin	1388	2576	1251	3701	3953	2975	2617	2271	2763	1608	2001	2553	4567	3436	3940	2083	944	547	242

4. A BRIEF CHINESE CHRONOLOGY

Xia	c. 21st century-16th century B.C.
Shang	c. 16th century-11th century B.C.
Zhou	c. 11th century-221 B.C.
Western Zhou	c. 11th century-770 B.C.
Eastern Zhou	770-221 B.C.
Spring and Autumn Period	770-476 B.C.
Warring States Period	475-221 B.C.
Qin	221-207 B.C.
Han	206 B.C.-A.D. 220
Western Han	206 B.C.-A.D. 24
Eastern Han	25-220
Three Kingdoms	220-280
Wei	220-265
Shu	221-263
Wu	222-280
Jin	265-420
Western Jin	265-316
Eastern Jin	317-420
Southern and Northern Dynasties	420-589
Southern Dynasties	420-589
Song	420-479
Qi	479-502
Liang	502-557
Chen	557-589

Northern Dynasties	386-581
Northern Wei	386-534
Eastern Wei	534-550
Western Wei	535-557
Northern Qi	550-577
Northern Zhou	557-581
Sui	581-618
Tang	618-907
Five Dynasties	907-960
Song	960-1279
Northern Song	960-1127
Southern Song	1127-1279
Liao	916-1125
Kin	1115-1234
Yuan	1271-1368
Ming	1368-1644
Qing	1644-1911
Republic of China	1912-1949
People's Republic of China	founded in 1949

5. TIME DIFFERENCE BETWEEN MAJOR CITIES IN THE WORLD

(12 o'clock Noon, Greenwich Mean Time)

City	Local Time	City	Local Time
Beijing	20:00	London	12:00
San Francisco	4:00	Conakry	12:00
Mexico City	6:00	Accra	12:00
Guatemala City	6:00	Bamako	12:00
Havana	7:00	Dakar	12:00
Panama City	7:00	Algiers	12:00
Bogota	7:00	Brazzaville	13:00
Lima	7:00	Tirana	13:00
Washington	7:00	Stockholm	13:00
New York	7:00	Vienna	13:00
Caracas	7:30	Warsaw	13:00
Santiago (Chile)	8:00	Rome	13:00
Buenos Aires	9:00	Prague	13:00
Montevideo	9:00	Paris	13:00
Reykjavik	11:00	Geneva	13:00

City	Local Time	City	Local Time
Budapest	13:00	New Delhi	17:30
Belgrade	13:00	Bombay	17:30
Berlin	13:00	Dacca	18:00
Sofia	14:00	Rangoon	18:30
Damascus	14:00	Phnom Penh	19:00
Ankara	14:00	Bangkok	19:00
Cairo	14:00	Hanoi	19:00
Lusaka	14:00	Ulan Bator	19:00
Capetown	14:00	Djakarta	19:30
Bucharest	14:00	Singapore	19:30
Helsinki	14:00	Manila	20:00
Baghdad	15:00	Irkutsk	20:00
Nairobi	15:00	Pyongyang	21:00
Dar es Salaam	15:00	Tokyo	21:00
Moscow	15:00	Osaka	21:00
Teheran	15:30	Canberra	22:00
Karachi	17:00	Wellington	24:00
Colombo	17:30		